POWER BI

*Essential Beginner's Guide
to Power BI*

Liam Damien

Table of Contents

Introduction

Power BI is a business intelligence solution that brings together all your business data in one place so you can understand and operate it as an integrated whole and thus gains valuable insight.

In the past, you may have used Excel to organize data and visualize it in a basic chart. The problem was that this was time-consuming due to the need to pull information from various applications and databases manually.

With Power BI, this "headache" is automatically resolved by feeding a central system with data from multiple sources. That way, you can quickly organize the information you need to build charts that can provide you a better perception of the true meaning of your business data.

Because Power BI is hosted on the cloud, you can access your data and graphs from anywhere, anytime, on any device. You can even share and work on real-time teaming directly from Power BI.

To let you know more about Power BI, we have prepared this eBook, from which you will learn why it matters, how it works, and the benefits of using it.

This eBook is for beginners in Power BI. It will help you build your first report on the tool and will properly introduce you to this new world of possibilities. This guide will be developed entirely from the Desktop version of Power BI, so if you do not already have the program installed on your PC, download the latest version of the Desktop version of Power BI.

The broader goal of this book is to help novice users of Power BI, as well as users of Power Query add-ins on Excel and Power Pivot, to learn these great tools. It is expected that the toolkit will someday become a more lightweight and humane alternative to the current official Power BI Help.

This eBook supports the placement of links to detailed discussions of the topics described in the official Power BI Help or other related resources.

Good reading!

Chapter 1

The Basic Of Business Intelligence & Power BI

Business Intelligence (BI)

With the aim of being able to survive in today's competitive business world, companies must highlight in their internal structure the real value of the information, and to do this, different strategies and technological tools are used to store data relevant to the development. Effective organization, which serves at the time of conducting relevant analyzes, will improve competitiveness.

To be more precise, all the strategies and procedures that are implemented in a company based on its correct administration and management of its processes are included in the concept known as Business Intelligence (BI), which in Spanish is known as Business Intelligence.

What is BI?

BI is a concept that refers to all those activities that a company carries out in order to collect more than valuable information, mainly around the development of its competitors within the market.

This data collection, which is carried out through different software systems specially designed for this, allows analysis and evaluation of the different fluctuations presented by the current market, and thus have results that guide commercial activities of the company.

The objective is not to lose money and at the same time, achieve real competitiveness within the commercial niche in which the organization in question is located. Hence the significant relevance of the data analysis that allows the company to obtain accurate results in different aspects of the market, with which it is possible to establish the correct strategies for the immediate future.

For this reason, the activities included in the so-called BI include different types of analysis and evaluations, which are carried out on competition, the market and industry, that is, information is collected around these three levels, in order to have accurate data in the face of the imminent development of a new business strategy.

Outsource or own platform?
To this end, companies usually outsource, that is, hire a service agency that collects the information, although other companies, usually the largest, including a group of employees in their stable staff dedicated exclusively to business intelligence.

Of course, the investment costs are not the same in both cases but, of course, a medium or small company usually hires this service out to third parties, since the investment is less than what it would be in the case of having an in house area dedicated to BI.

How is the BI process?

When the process begins, those who carry out the work will in principle collect all the data related to the internal procedures of the organization, with the objective of being able to analyze said information subsequently and, based on that information, establish what aspects the company should improve from the inside.

In this regard, we could point out that depending on the complexity of the system, the solutions provided by BI focus on reports and statistical analyses. On the one hand, with regard to reports, this platform allows the company to have predefined reports tailored to each organization, including online analytical process systems of the O LAP type.

With regard to statistical analyzes, the solutions provided by BI include the possibility of accessing short, medium, and long term forecasts, establishing a Data Mining system, that is, data and process mining, and of course, the optimization of the use of resources.

After this evaluation, the information that will begin to be collected will be exterior information - that is to say, the BI area must collect data about different aspects external to the company, including public records of other companies in the same sector, market data, customer surveys, and other relevant info.

BI Results

In this way, it is possible in principle to establish which are the true competitors of the company and take information about the strategies used by them, and then have this valuable information when making decisions upon the development of the company's own strategies. At this point, of course, the opinion of customers and consumers, in general, will also be remarkably relevant, together with which market analysis and surveys offer great value.

With the information collected and the analyses performed, a company can then create new ideas for new businesses, generate different initiatives, establish more appropriate marketing campaigns, since it has a more precise idea of the needs and desires of customers, and at the same time the company staff know how to compete with companies in the same market.

Advantages of BI systems

That is why BI business intelligence systems are many and varied for companies, especially in today's competitive market. Through the information, they provide the possibility for the organization to accelerate and improve decision-making becomes easier, which is essential for the effective development of the company.

At the same time, BI systems make it possible to optimize internal business processes, including a notable increase in operational efficiency, and thus improve productivity.

Simultaneously, with the collection and analysis of external data, BI systems allow companies to obtain a real competitive advantage over their commercial rivals, and this information also helps in the identification of new market trends and recognizing and attacking those problems of the Business that need to be resolved.

The Career of a Business Intelligence Analyst

Business intelligence is a specialization highly valued by the market. Understand Your Challenges and Differentials.

In the digitally globalized world, the most precious asset is information. Organizations are increasingly looking for integrity and quality data to assist in strategic decision-making and value creation because they recognize data as an asset of the organization supporting business decision-making. Intelligence analysis results are used to develop predictions of behavior or recommended actions to be taken by leaders of an organization, country, or industry.

Due to this growing need, intelligent and automated processes that ensure the delivery of information in a safe and reliable manner are essential. To make this possible, there is the BI Analyst. He is the one who can answer questions like these: How should this information be collected? Is it possible to consolidate information from different sources? How should it be treated and stored? Are there appropriate tools? How do you guarantee the quality? How to develop performance and automated processes. How to ensure the governance of this data.

The answers to these questions and many more will be found in this book, and are intended to support you in deciding whether or not to pursue the career as a Business Intelligence Analyst.

Typical Issues Faced by BI Analyst
Organizations today need the information to stay competitive and deliver value to their customers and partners. However, in order to generate reliable and quality information, the business intelligence analyst must address the following issues:

- Organization's culture;

- Business uniqueness;

- Understanding of the needs of the organization;

- Multiple sources of data;

- Diversity of systemic technologies;

- Availability of users;

- Technology investment;

- Application security;

- Compliance with regulatory agencies;

- Solutions that do not use industry standards;

- Need for integrations with various legacy solutions within the organization and partners;

- Problems defining the scope of projects related to business and architectural requirements;

Behavioral Profile of Business Intelligence Analysis Professional

A professional who wants to become a BI Analyst needs to develop skills to solve the challenges that the position presents:

- Communication: Knowing how to express and make yourself understood are crucial points for success. Have clarity in the definition of premises for the execution of activities, the ability to communicate and define scopes and risks, seeking to present Intelligence solutions in a direct and objective language, which both the sponsor and the interested parties understand.

- Peacemaker: The BI Analyst has an arduous but glorious task: he is the one who bridges the gap between sponsor and stakeholders. He is the person who can translate the business rules in the technological world. He is responsible for aligning expectations of who pays for the project with who uses the project deliverables.

- Leadership. The BI Analyst must have a leadership profile. It is he who will drive the solutions and drive the people involved. He needs to be the conductor of this orchestra in order for everything to work out. He should give proper and safe advice and information, as well as guiding the team and all interested parties.

- Technical knowledge. The BI Analyst must have comprehensive technical knowledge, not just the solution design. He is also responsible for ensuring that the solution is developed within the best way, with the best possible effort, and with the right technology.

- Attitude (Make it happen). The BI Analyst is not a mere contributor or participant, but he is effectively the one who makes things happen. It is he who has logical reasoning, he who defines processes, designs solution models, and he who holds business and technical knowledge, so without him, things do not work.

Required areas of technical knowledge

The professional needs to master relevant areas to be able to perform the activities of this career, since the BI Analyst must have knowledge in the following areas:

- **People Management:** Professionals need to master personal communication through leadership, negotiation, and conflict management techniques. The BI Analyst must also be able to establish strategic planning to seek self-awareness, seeking to map the strengths, weaknesses, opportunities, and threats that are inherent in any business intelligence project.

- **Business Intelligence, Business Analytics, and Big Data**: Intelligence analytics develop using a wide range of available information sources, and assess information to meet the needs of decision-makers and leaders to assist in decision making. The BI Analyst needs to have a solid understanding of the key technologies that currently deliver business conditions to explore and evaluate information. Business Intelligence, Business

Analytics, and Big Data are today the conceptual and technological pillars that drive information management strategies in today's world. The BI Analyst needs to have in his or her professional portfolio as much mastery of these concepts and technologies as possible to address the best solution for an organization.

- **Data Governance**: When an organization can transform data into information, it becomes the most valuable asset of the organization. Data management has the function of guiding and caring for all data models created in new projects and for maintaining and updating the quality of old data models. The growing concern with privacy, security, and effective use of data has made information management one of the most critical activities of organizations. The BI Analyst must ensure the governance of an organization's data, as data is its most important asset.

- **Information Security**: The professional who assumes the role of Intelligence Analyst should have a notion about information security, as they will work directly with the clients' databases, which have confidential information about the Organization's business.

- **Knowledge in business strategies**: Professionals who master the knowledge of business areas and seek alignment between the solutions to be developed and the objectives of organizations will succeed in their projects.

Skills

A professional who craves the role of BI Analyst needs to keep in mind which technical skills will be most required for this profile. In this sense, we can list the following as essential:

- Produce satisfactory technical and business results: BI analysts cannot be content with unsatisfactory results and should always seek continuous improvement of technical deliverables and components used in solution projects.

- Possess Strategic Business Vision: Aligning what organizations' business areas expect from IT is one of the biggest challenges for a BI Analyst. Delivering a value-adding solution that is clearly aligned to support organizations' primary business processes is their primary goal.

- Facing the problems generated in the project: The BI Analyst must be the one who cannot be afraid of the problems created in the solution of projects. You should always face them head-on, assessing their possible root causes as well as contingency and definitive solutions throughout the solution project.

- Influencing, Collaborating, and Democratizing Decisions: The BI Analyst should know how to listen to his team when building solution architecture. Team involvement is critical because everyone needs to believe in what will be proposed. However, more than one path will emerge to choose from, and this is when the Architect needs to take over and guide the team toward what they believe is the best way to achieve the best-expected results for the solution project.

- Innovate: The BI Analyst needs to be open to innovations and market trends. He must be one of the professionals who most closely follow the technological news released by the market. It is important to keep in mind which solution components are up, which are out of use, and which should be avoided when building solution architecture.

- Seek Continuous Learning: The BI Analyst should establish feedback mechanisms to identify which areas of knowledge need improvement. In addition, there is no frozen knowledge because the professional who considers himself senior and assumes a comfort zone does not survive in the current job market.

- Accept legacy systems: Today's organizations already have a diverse application infrastructure, and the BI Analyst should know market products for solutions such as ERP, CRM, Identity Management, Business Process Management (BPMS) solutions because their solutions will certainly have to communicate with this entire technological ecosystem.

Tasks and activities that the business intelligence specialist performs

The primary goal of a BI Analyst is to be able to deliver solutions that meet business expectations but without neglecting architectural requirements. This means that he is responsible for ensuring that the solution delivers customer-value functional requirements along with security, scalability, availability, performance, and usability.

A BI Analyst spends most of his time in meetings with the development team and his clients. At these meetings, he is responsible for communicating drivers and directing the team on architectural decisions that support all components chosen for the solution. This defense is made on both the technical and business fronts, where there are cost, time, and scope set boundaries for determining which path to take.

Among the activities of a BI Analyst, we can highlight the list below:

- Identify and model business requirements;
- Define and direct architectures for the solution;
- Search for new solutions and innovations.
- Perform effort and time estimates to support the project manager;
- Perform PoC (Proof of Concept) to validate reference implementations;
- Select solution components such as frameworks, databases, application servers, etc. for the solution;
- Ensure that the proposed architecture is being followed;
- Support the development team in problem-solving;
- Attend technical meetings with the team;
- Attend meetings with clients;

- Be responsible for all technical project decisions;
- Establish criteria and components for solution security;
- Manage technical risks;

It is also important to note that a BI Analyst does not live on an island. That is, in defining the architecture of a solution, the BI Analyst is influenced by other roles. For example, business areas affect you directly by setting business goals. The technical area directly impacts it with governance definitions, such as establishing partner products to be used.

Comparison with other professional profiles

The choice of a career directed to studies to work as a BI Analyst must be evaluated very clearly, as we currently have several roles that work with Technology and Information. Some of these roles have shaded areas with the responsibilities of a BI Analyst and others not.

Many people initially have the idea that a BI Analyst is similar to a Data Scientist. But their profiles are far from being this. They may be complementary.

Observing below, we have made a comparison between the profile of a BI Analyst and a Data Scientist through two polar graphs that address the dimensions involved in each profile.

It should be noted that a BI Analyst must have a very strong background in Management and Information, i.e., knowledge in the following:

- Business Intelligence Architecture;

- Information extraction and processing processes;

- People management;

- Technologies for information management;

Already the Data Scientist must have a very strong background in Technology and Data Science, i.e., knowledge in the following:

- Manipulation of large masses of data;

- Big data;

- Software solution engineering;

- Information Technology;

When choosing a BI Analyst career, it is important to keep in mind that, like many other professions, it will not be an easy task. Professionals who have gone through different roles such as Business Analyst, Systems Analyst, Technical Leaders, or DBAs will certainly have a background that will facilitate this walk.

Success for an information technology professional is in their pursuit of knowledge and improvement. They are always updating and innovating.

It can be said that the profession of BI Analyst is the top of a pyramid that will require a lot of dedication, technical knowledge, and initiative, as it is the exact area, Information Technology, which is one of the most coveted careers today.

The Power BI

This section aims to highlight some features of Power BI, the possibilities it offers, its applications, and its target audience. Briefly, these points will be raised to open your mind to this technology that has already spread and conquered many professionals and amateurs.

Power BI is a collection of services, applications, and connectors. That is, it makes it possible to connect to your data wherever it is, allows you to make filters, create compelling visualizations, and share with anyone.

And to you?

Whether you are a student, salesperson, or team manager who wants to share data from an Excel spreadsheet, for example, Power BI makes this possible very clearly, allowing all stakeholders to understand the business ideas demonstrated there.

If you are a developer or an IT Pro who works with real-time Azure SQL Data Warehouse tables, combined with other databases, and with continuous delivery source codes, Power BI is also your tool. In this case, you can create a data set that monitors manufacturing progress, for example.

With these two short examples, you can see that for you to develop graphical analysis in Power BI, there is no need for a unique type of professional niche or knowledge. Anyone can work with the tool and do the analysis that best suits their business.

Why POWER BI?

The advantages of Microsoft Power BI tool in relation to others in the market are based on a friendlier user interface, the previous existence of storage systems and institutional data repository, adaptability to mobile devices and the ease of connecting to other Microsoft products through the links that the University has for it, through the platform Office 365.

Power BI consists of a Windows desktop application called Desktop version of Power BI, an online SaaS service (software as a service) called Power BI service, and applications Power BI mobile available for Windows phones and tablets, and for Android & iOS devices.

What is Power BI?

Power BI, in general prospect, is a combination of applications, connectors, and software services that work mutually to convert distinct sources of data into coherent, dynamic, visually appealing, and interactive information. Whether it's a local or cloud-based hybrid data collection store or a simple Excel spreadsheet, Power BI lets you connect easily to the sources of your data, visualize (or explore) the most important facts and share this with whomever you wish.

Power BI, as a tool, is easy and fast; able to create quick information from your local database or Excel spreadsheet. However, **** is also stable and has a business-friendly functionality, ready for real-time analysis, in-depth modeling, and custom development. Therefore, it can become your personal tool for creating reports and visualization, as well as acting as the decision engine and analysis that drives projects in divisions, groups, or entire businesses.

The elements of Power BI

Power BI comprises a desktop application for Windows known as the Desktop version of Power BI, a SaaS service (software as service) online called Power BI service and Power BI mobile available applications for phones and Windows tablets, as well as for iOS and Android devices.

These three components, Desktop, the online service, and the one for mobile devices, are intended to allow users to generate, share and use business information in a way that is most effective for their role.

Adapting Power BI to your role

It is possible that the way you are using Power BI depends upon the role you are playing in a team or project. Therefore, other people with other roles may be using Power BI in a different way, which is normal.

For example, it may be the case that you use the web service of Power BI primarily, while your co-worker, dedicated to processing numbers and creating business reports, uses the Desktop version of Power BI (and publishes Desktop reports in the Power PI service so that you could see them). On the other hand, another partner who is dedicated to sales could mainly use the Power BI mobile application to monitor the progress of their sales quotas then deepen the details of potential new customers.

You could also use each individual Power BI element at separate times, based on your objective or your role in a given team or project.

You may see the progress of inventory and production on a dashboard in real-time in the service section and can use the Desktop service of Power BI to generate reports for your team on customer membership statistics. The way of your Power BI use may depend on the service or feature of Power BI that is best for you.

However, you will have full Power BI at your disposal; for this reason, it is so attractive and flexible.

We will explain these three core elements: desktop, online service, and applications for mobile devices, in more detail in the next chapters of this eBook. In the next chapters, you will also learn to generate reports in the Desktop version of Power BI, sharing them in the online service and analyzing them in-depth on your mobile device.

The Power BI workflow

A common workflow in the Power BI starts in the Desktop version, where reports are created. These reports are then published in the web service of Power BI and, after that, shared so that Power BI Mobile applications users can use that information.

It doesn't always have to be done that way, but we will use the flow in order to help you discover the different Power BI parts and the way they complement each other.

Now that you have read an overview of this book, you know what Power BI is, and you know its three core components, so let's see how to use Power BI.

Getting started

Power BI is built on top of the following blocks:

- Visualizations - Visual representations of the data;
- Dataset - Data collection used by the tool to create the visualizations;
- Reports - Collection of visuals of a dataset;
- Dashboards - Single page collection of visuals, created based on reports;
- Blocks - Single view found on a Dashboard.

The common Power BI workflow is based on the following sequence: Create a report on - Desktop version of power BI, publish it to the Power BI service, and share it with other stakeholders.

Remember, this is just one of the most common usage streams.

In this flow, to create a report, you must first enter data into Power BI. Available data sources range from Excel files to Azure databases. In addition, Power BI also connects to software services such as SaaS providers or cloud services like Salesforce, Google Analytics, and Facebook.

If you paid attention to the services shown above, you should have noticed Github. That is, you can create a dashboard for viewing pull requests made in Github code, contributors, time spent, etc. Additionally, you can ask questions about your data through natural language. Power BI will take care of creating a real-time visualization with the most frequently asked questions.

Business Intelligence - Data Cleansing and Transformation
Power BI doesn't just stop at data entry and reporting and visualization. As its name implies, it is a great Business Intelligence tool. Anyone who has had contact with BI knows that simply entering data does not solve the problems of data analysis.

One of the greatest difficulties in handling BI data is cleaning and transforming it. When dealing with a large amount of data, it is impossible to use all raw data. The correct thing is to do the cleaning, that is, remove from our database those that are not essential in generating information.

After this cleanup, it is often necessary to transform the data, which means changing the format in which it was acquired to formats in which it can be worked and, finally, generating information relevant to the business.

Power BI has a Query Editor, a feature that can format and transform data to make it ready for use in the templates and visualizations you want to create. In addition, Power BI is capable of cleaning up data that has been irregularly formatted, which ensures that you only work with business-sensitive data.

Business Intelligence - Data Modeling

Often the data used in reporting comes from a variety of sources, and in order for you to make the data work efficiently, you need to make this data work together.

To solve this problem, you must create a relationship between the data. This relationship will allow Power BI to understand how the tables relate. Relationship View is where you will be able to do this.

To accomplish this task, you can add or remove relationships simply and intuitively drag and drop. You can also manage cardinality options. That is, define many-to-one and one-to-one relationships.

In addition, you can create columns based on calculations performed between data. That is, Power BI not only limits you to working with the data you enter but also generates new dynamic data based on the entries you choose. All to optimize the tool for the specific need of your business.

Views

The visualizations part is one of the most attractive facets of Power BI. Here you can generate almost any visualization, just choose the one that best suits your needs.

Map

Here you can use geographic maps for data visualization.

Arrays and Tables

As stated many times throughout the article, Power BI adapts to any type of user. Often, however, matrices and tables succinctly summarize the information we need to visualize. Therefore, this display format is also available.

Scatter Plots

This type of chart is widely used when comparing two different quantities.

Funnel and waterfall charts

Cascade plots are commonly used to demonstrate the behavior of a specific value over time. The funnel chart, on the other hand, is used to demonstrate changes made throughout a specific process.

Single Number Card Meters

Typically these indicators serve to track a single KPI or metric over time. In Power BI, you can set these values dynamically by setting minimum, maximum, and goal.

Modify colors in visual graphics

Often colors act as warning codes for humans. Red usually indicates danger, yellow attention, and green, tranquility, for example. Power BI lets you use colors the way you want.

Shapes, text boxes and images

Although dynamic assets are extremely useful, sometimes static information is required. Power BI provides us with text boxes and images that serve as static elements to enhance the visual design of reports.

Formatting and layout

This item lets you control page layouts, such as size and orientation. There are predefined fixed sizes, but the tool also allows you to work with dynamic formats.

Group interactions between views

When working with scatter plots, it is not interesting to limit the data to a specific segment, as this will undermine the understanding of the plot. To solve such problems, Power BI lets you control the flow of interactions between visuals. That is, the selection of specific segments need not necessarily affect the others.

R

Are you a programmer in R? In Power BI, you can create statistical and analytical analysis and create visuals with R integration through the R script editor panel.

Summary

Now that you have gained a brief understanding of Power BI's possibilities, audience, and applications, you can decide how to make the best use of it for your benefit, for your business, or your team. But Power BI doesn't stop there; there are many other possibilities for integration, visualization, and applications.

Chapter 2

A smarter Insight Into Microsoft Power BI

Power BI

We know Microsoft Power BI is the tool that will help you create rich visual objects, based on your company or business data. The process is very simple: first, a data collection is done. Then stories are built in a simple way. Simply drag the selected data, and you will have elements to create custom panels. In them, you will mount all kinds of information related to your company, whose background data will have been collected in the previous steps. If you want, you can share these panels with the rest of your company.

Information about Power BI

Microsoft BI is the perfect tool if you want to monitor everything that concerns your company or business in a very graphic way. It consists of an online service that allows the creation of panels and mosaics, to make the exhaustive monitoring of the elements in which you are interested much more visual.

In its new version, it incorporates an extra tool called the Desktop version of Power BI. With it, you can generate very detailed reports based on data from different sources, which you can reach using the Query Editor. It is a really easy-to-use program, whose results will give you the option to make colorful reports of what you want. The format can be shaped as you wish, as well as graphics, colors, and mosaics. When finished, you can easily send these reports to the network, to insert them into your Microsoft Power BI tool and use them as support for the analysis you carry out.

It is the solution of Microsoft that will help you to approach, unify, analyze and know as never before, the universe of data and information of your organization, through incredible visual objects enriched and interactive that will facilitate understanding of the state of the situation of a deal.

Thoroughly visualize your business. Unlock business data and discover the potential of your business lines that otherwise remained hidden or unexploited. Evaluate sales figures, marketing actions, financial situation, operations, production, after-sales, as well as those other areas and departments you need to examine.

Manage and analyze in a centralized way, in real-time, all your data from a global perspective, to the detailed one: No matter where you are, or the device you have at any time. Simply place yourself at the center of the information that is vital to your business and move on to making the best decisions and sharing them with your team members.

What is Power BI?

It will help you with the consolidation of your organization's data in a similar, standardized, and simple way; allowing you to present them through spectacular visual objects, graphics, and infographics.

Build, edit, publish, and share your own panels and reports, choosing which graphic element you want your data to represent.

Know in general or in detail the status of your company. Browse through the information, being able to integrate more than 65 data sources. Whether provided by internal or external databases.

Make amazing presentations from a mobile, tablet, workstation, or laptop. It does not matter where you are and what device you consult your information with.

Access a greater understanding of your business, through questions with natural language in Power BI, through your own dashboards and reports. Ask in your own language the situation of your sales; finance, marketing campaigns; investment and returns from its presence in social networks; operations; After-sales services and even their production lines, through the data provided by third-party systems.

Simply analyze and enrich the knowledge you have about your organization in a different, intelligent, and more attractive way, allowing you to make better decisions about information in real-time.

Power BI features

Power BI has functions that complement Excel, as well as others that are based on the cloud with excellent potential.

Excel add-ins are as follows:

- Power Pivot: It is the engine that runs all the calculations that are displayed visually interactively in the reports generated by you.

- Power Query: Transforms raw data into useful tables to be used by Power Pivot or Excel.

- Power View: Tool with which you can visualize data, exploring them in a very simple, highly visual and intuitive way.

- Power Map: Tool to visualize geospatial data, in 3D. It is an Excel add-on with which you can geo-locate, explore, and interact with geographic and temporal data.

- The cloud-based services are the ones you will find below:

- Refreshing, sharing, and managing the data sources: With this module, you can upload all the data and keep it online connected to each other.

- Natural Q&A Query Language: This amazing module will allow you to query data with conditions in natural language. The system will search for the answer in all the data tables, and in a few seconds, it will be displayed on the screen in the format you want: table, graph, number, etc. It is ideal for saving time: from now on, you will avoid searching certain data among hundreds of tables.

- Dashboards: This is the section where you can create graphic panels as interactive reports. It will do it in a simple way, while in the background, they will be writing codes in HTML5.

- Native apps for mobile phones and tablets: If you have iOS or Windows as an operating system on your smartphone or tablet, you can use all Microsoft BI applications from anywhere.

Power BI functionalities
- Quick start: Publish and access your panels and reports in seconds and few steps.

- Easy: No technical knowledge is required to create custom reports and dashboards. Simply create, update, publish, and share for greater collaboration with others.

- Centralize information: Unify data from different sources in the same report and dashboard, without having to change applications.

- Data sources: Take advantage of the ability to integrate data sources as different as those provided by:

  ✔ Salesforce,
  ✔ MailChimp,

- ✔ SAP BW,

- ✔ SAP HANA,

- ✔ MySQL,

- ✔ SQL Server,

- ✔ Teradata,

- ✔ Oracle,

- ✔ Google,

- ✔ Twitter,

- ✔ Facebook,

- ✔ Dynamics 365…. Up to 65 origins and growing.

- Real-time: Schedule the download of data for your key indicators as much as you need, to access updated information.

- Use your own language: Use the powerful Q&A functionality to get answers to the information you are looking for in Power BI as if speaking to someone else.

- Attractive graphics: Design your data with incredible and dynamic animation. Or if you like the traditional way, use regular graphics but in a way that is more attractive than usual.

- Geolocation: Learn about a flat or 3D map, the disposition of the data you want to know at the local, regional, or continental level.

- Collaboration: Share your reports to offer information to the members of your organization, facilitating the exchange of knowledge and approaches to problems, to face decision-making.

- Security: Establish profiles or access roles to information for each member of your organization.

- Mobile: There are native apps for tablets and mobile devices that run on the Android and iOS operating systems.

Power BI Modalities

- Power BI for Desktop: Use it for free for the integration of data sources, the modeling, and construction of your panels and reports, selecting and dragging the visual objects you want, for the representation, exploitation, and sharing of information.

- Power BI for Mobile: Download the free APP for viewing your panels and reports from mobile devices, whether Android or iOS. Access the information created and published previously, from a Tablet or Smartphone.

- Power BI Online: Access your panels and reports through a web address, which was provided at the time of publication. Consult, edit, and republish, from any computer other than your usual computer, with an Internet connection.

- The Pro version of Power BI: It is the license for administrators and users who need to integrate large amounts of data and consume them every hour. Install advanced visual elements, establish security profiles, and configure gateways, equipment creation, among other features.

- The Embedded version of Power BI: The most advanced service will allow you to manage huge amounts of data, generated in your industry to be published for example in web services or integrate data from external elements of the IoT type by accessing a higher level of knowledge of information from a spectacular graphic representation.

More information

There is a free version of Power BI, so that you can see, applied to your company, the fantastic advantages of using this Microsoft tool. You just have to register and start testing. It will have limitations that will not prevent you from knowing all the product options in depth. If you convince yourself and register, all of them will disappear, and you will have access to everything described above.

The desktop version of Power BI: Design and get attractive reports and dashboards, dragging the type of graphics you want to visualize, very easily on the canvas.

Power BI Mobile: Access your Power BI reports and dashboards from Windows Phone, iOS, and Android. Get a complete overview of your business with just one click.

Power BI mobile: Android, iPhone, and iPad applications

If you are one of those who go everywhere with your iPhone, you can now also go with the mobile application of Power BI for iPhone and iPod Touch.

In addition to viewing Power BI panels and reports, you can also add Power BI to Apple Watch and annotate and share an icon, report, or display. The Microsoft Power BI mobile app for iOS on iPad offers the mobile BI experience for Power BI, Power BI report server, and Reporting Services.

With direct mobile access and in the cloud, you can see the panels of the company and interact with them easily from anywhere. Explore panel data and share it with your classmates in text messages or email.

You can try Power BI and Reporting Services examples, even without registering. To do this, you must download the application. In addition, it will also be able to:

- Search content in Power BI mobile applications.

- Locate a panel or report.

- View reports, KPIs, and favorite panels.

With Power BI mobile, you can be connected from anywhere and at any time. Power BI applications for Windows, iOS, and Android will allow you to have a global view of your business data anywhere, anytime.

And there is no doubt, and today the mobile has become a fundamental work tool. A reality that is due in part to great mobility, collaborative work, and relocation in jobs, leads us to add the mobile to the list of tools of our day-to-day work.

Cloud services, as well as instant messaging and video conferencing, to give some examples, become vital in the daily operations of any company. All this is possible thanks to mobile applications, which allow us to use this software from our devices; whether mobile or tablets — being able to connect your company's data locally and in the cloud.

With Power BI mobile you can:
- Visualize. View reports and custom panels anywhere. Interact with the data easily in a touch experience optimized with the native Windows, iOS, and Android applications of Power BI.

- Be informed. Keep up with data controlled alerts. Discover important information in real-time and make decisions instantly.

- Share knowledge with your team. Share active reports and panels so that everyone is informed.

Android applications

The mobile application of Power BI for Android phones allows you to carry Power BI in your pocket, with updated and real mobile device access to the information of your company. In addition, you can view your KPI, the report server of Power BI and Reporting

Services reports directly on your phone. You can even detect a QR code with your Android phone and go directly to a Power BI panel or report.

This mobile application runs on various Android tablets and offers you tactile and updated mobile access to your company's information. On an Android tablet, the application of Power BI mobile displays the panels and reports as designed for the service of Power.

What else can you do?

- Connect up to 5 report servers (maximum) in order to see Power BI KPIs and reports that are organized in the folders or accumulated as favorites. You can also bookmark your favorite panels and reports, for quick access, along with your KPIs and favorite reports from Power BI report server and Reporting Services

- Explore examples of mobile applications without connection to the server. If you do not have access to a web portal of Reporting Services, you are still able to search the highlights of mobile reports, KPIs, and Reporting Services.

- Connect to a local server.

- Remove a connection to a report server.

It is possible to scan the QR code to get immediate access to the corresponding icon or report, directly from your phone, using the

Power BI application scanner or any other scanner installed on the phone.

iPhone applications

If you are one of those who go everywhere with your iPhone, you can now also go with the mobile app of Power BI for iPhone and iPod Touch.

In addition to viewing Power BI panels and reports, you can also add Power BI to Apple Watch and annotate and share an icon, report, or display. The Microsoft Power BI mobile app for iOS on iPad offers the mobile BI experience for Power BI, Power BI report server, and Reporting Services.

With direct mobile access and in the cloud, you can see the panels of the company and interact with them easily from anywhere. Explore panel data and share it with your classmates in text messages or email.

You can try Power BI and Reporting Services examples, even without registering. To do this, you must download the application. In addition, it will also be able to:

- Search content in Power BI mobile applications.

- Locate a panel or report.

- View reports, KPIs, and favorite panels.

IPad applications

On an iPad, Power BI mobile application will also show you the panels and reports as designed for Power BI service. You can configure data alerts in Power BI mobile application to receive a notification when data changes in a panel beyond the set limits. Alerts work on icons with a particular number, like cards and meters, yet not by running data. You are able to set up data alerts on the mobile device, then see them in the service of Power BI, and vice versa.

In addition, you can filter a report by its geographic location, by examining Power BI reports on your mobile device.

Remember that to enable this function, you must activate the location tags for which these three conditions must be met:

1. The person who created the report in the Desktop mode of Power BI classified the geographic data for at least one column, such as City, State, or Country or region.

2. You are in one of the locations that have data in that column.

3. Use one of these mobile devices:
    - ✔ iOS, (iPhone, (iPad or iPod).
    - ✔ Android tablet or phone.
    - ✔ Windows 10 phones (other Windows 10 devices, such as tablets and computers, do not support geographic filtering).

Power BI is the perfect tool if you want to monitor everything that concerns your company or business in a very graphic way. Build, edit, publish, and share your own panels and reports, choosing which graphic element you want your data to represent.

Microsoft Power BI Embedded Licenses

The Embedded Power BI is one of Azure's services. You are only charged usage fees (per user session and time), and when using Azure Portal, the user who sees the report is not charged anything and is not required to have an Azure subscription. Therefore, we can say that there are no Embedded Power BI licenses as such, but rather it would be the Azure license that entitles the charging of sessions for the Embedded service of Power BI.

Cost of Embedded Power BI licenses

Sessions solve the cost of licenses in the Microsoft Embedded Power BI usage model. This means, in this case, that the developer acquires sessions for the use he makes, for example. These sessions are added to the corresponding subscription.

Sessions are user interactions with Embedded Power BI reports. Each time an Embedded Power BI report is shown to a user, a session is initiated, and a session will be charged to the subscription holder. Sessions are billed at a flat rate, regardless of the number of visual elements in a report or how often the content of the report is updated. A session ends when the user closes the report or one hour after the session starts, whichever comes first.

Power BI Embedded is billed and implemented through the Azure Portal and is aimed at independent software manufacturers and companies that integrate panels into applications whose use is intended for third parties.

Types of licenses

We can talk about three types of licenses when working with Power BI:

The Desktop Service of Power BI

It is free and whose functions allow you to:

- Get connected to numerous data sources,
- Prepare and clean the data with visual tools,
- Create and analyze amazing reports with customized visualizations,
- Publish in the online service of Power BI.
- Embed on public websites

The Pro version of Power BI

With this Power BI Pro version you can:

It provides all the fascinating features of Power BI, in addition to other features, such as increased storage capacity, scheduled data updates more frequently than once a day, dynamic data sources with full interactivity, groups and much more, such as:

- Create panels that offer a real-time 360-degree view of the company.

- Keep data updated automatically, including sources in local storage.
- Collaborate on shared data.
- Audit and regulate how data is accessed and how it is used.
- Package the content and distribute it to the users with the applications.

Power BI Premium

This license is based on capacity, while Power BI Pro is a user license that provides dedicated support to operate the Power BI service for your organization or team, offering you more reliable performance and higher data volumes. Power BI Premium also allows the widespread distribution of content without the need to acquire licenses for each user.

To start using the Power BI Premium capability, you need to assign a work area to capacity. When a work area is backed by Premium capability, you can enjoy the benefits of Power BI Premium.

If an application has the support of the Premium capability, that is, it was published from a work area of the application that is currently assigned to Premium, any user of the organization can use that published application, regardless of the license that has assigned. This means that even users of the free Power BI level can use these distributed applications.

Power BI Embedded Features

The primary function of Power BI Embedded is undoubtedly to boost data in applications with inserted analysis. That means you can use it to easily add impactful, completely interactive reports into the apps in a cost-effective and scalable way.

But you can also:

- Test and implement business applications with the virtual machines of Azure, SQL databases, and Azure managed disks while offering vast ease of use and excellent network capacity with Load Balancer.
- Create personalized mobile experiences based on the behavior and interests of its customers using Application Service and Xamarin, Azure Cosmos DB, Traffic Manager, and HockeyApp.
- Get Power BI Premium information about your data to make data-based decisions and to create better experiences by using Machine Learning, HDInsight, and Data Analytics.

Power BI Pro & Contact Center

Power BI Pro enhances the customer service quality of your contact center, discover the advantages of Power BI Pro for the contact center.

What is Power BI Pro?

It is a business analytics service on the cloud, a tool that offers a unique view of the most important data of your business.

Thanks to this service, you can monitor the state of your company at all times and in real-time, through a very visual active panel. This panel gives you the possibility, thanks to the Desktop version of Power BI, to create rich interactive reports.

Power BI Pro adds all the features of the free version of Power BI and additional sharing and collaboration features.

The main difference between a user of the free version and another of the Pro version lies in sharing and collaboration.

Only users of the Pro version can publish content in application work areas, consume applications, share panels, and subscribe to dashboards and reports.

Power BI Pro functionalities
Power BI Pro is very suitable for those users who publish reports, share panels or collaborate with colleagues in work areas. But it also has numerous additional features such as:

- Analyze data in Excel or Desktop version of power BI Power BI Pro functionalities
- Share with Excel web application technical support
- Share panels and collaborate with application work areas
- See the shared content
- Integrate content with Microsoft Teams
- Create panels that offer a real-time 360-degree view of the company
- Keep data updated automatically, including sources in local storage
- Collaborate on shared data

- Audit and regulate how data is accessed and how it is used
- Package content and distribute it to users with applications

For clarifications between the Power BI Pro and Premium licenses, consult the frequently asked questions for help on the Microsoft website.

Advantages of Power BI Pro in Contact Centers

Undoubtedly, the main advantage that the Power BI Pro service provides to any contact center lies in its ability to enhance customer service units, without the need for extensive resources or investments.

How does Power BI Pro enhance customer service quality? This business intelligence tool will provide your organization with excellent quality in the attention and treatment of its customers. It gives you a clearly differential advantage and is simple to implement. Power BI structures and organizes your data. If the data is not structured, it is practically impossible to find the information we need. But there are also some other benefits such as:

End the chaos by working for your entire team in tune

Train your team to make quick and safe decisions with a single view of your company. The Power BI Groups enables you to collaborate with key participants to ensure that everyone uses the correct data.

Faster service

Calls will be resolved much earlier as it will be easier to access the information. Your customers will reduce waiting times and be more satisfied.

More productivity in the resolution of incidents

A more effective service, the conflicts will be resolved better and faster.

Your training is simpler and less expensive

By using an integrated platform with the main Microsoft office tools that most of your workers will be familiar with, the training will be faster and cheaper.

All these advantages are carried out through functions such as desktops integrated with a CRM, billing, spreadsheets, etc. integrated for a 360° view of the incidence. Workflows that automate repetitive tasks minimizing the need to enter data in duplicate. Predefined reports for reporting activities and many more specific functions for your contact center.

Summary

You know the complete tool for managing a business is business intelligence. These services collect and analyze the data and information of the environment of your organization, obtaining in a methodical and structured way the critical information; both internal and external. This helps in decision-making and strategic orientation.

The business intelligence applied to contact centers should focus on customer management since contact centers handle an infinity of information.

(This information comes from different sources: from telephone equipment, CRM systems, audio recordings of calls made, screen recordings and stored applications)

The handling of all this information is impossible without a suitable tool that:

- Capture this information, organize and manage it. So this correctly managed information will allow you to transform that data into intelligence with a lot of commercial and operational value.

Contact centers must use a BI (Business Intelligence) tool for the proper use of their data. In this way, this data can be converted into relevant information that will allow you to create an efficient commercial and operational management plan.

Chapter 3

Microsoft Power BI; Your First Steps

Through examples, based on a magazine sales scenario, you will be shown how to get started with working with the Microsoft Power BI tool. A model will be built considering the obtaining of raw data, going through the transformation phase, and finally, presenting the information treated in a dashboard, containing some of the various types of graphic components available in the tool.

From previous chapters, we already know that Power BI is a Microsoft tool for presenting information by creating dashboards and dashboards. Its use is ideal for analysts, directors, and managers, among others who need to build and present information in an integrated and dynamic way.

Although the larger target is the information presentation layer, it is also possible to perform data extract, transform, and load (ETL). Natively, Power BI enables connection to various data sources, thus allowing the creation of an integrated environment with data from various sources of information, ranging from a simple Excel spreadsheet to data from social networks.

By registering at Microsoft with a corporate account, you can create a project and make it available on the Internet or access it through smartphones. However, this article will use the desktop version of Power BI, as this version does not require the use of a corporate account. The desktop version of Power BI can be downloaded for free from the website described in the Links section.

According to Microsoft itself, Power BI is a business analytics solution that enables you to perform information analysis and share ideas. Power BI dashboards provide a broad, integrated view for business users so they can see their most important metrics. Information can be updated in real-time and can be available on multiple devices.

Creating a project is quite simple, there are more than 50 connections to various types of data sources, made available in a very simplified way through predefined forms that help to connect with them. To assemble the information presentation panel, it is possible to use several native visual graphic components, as well as a very active community that develops and customizes new components. From them, you can create compelling reports that effectively convey the desired message.

A project in Power BI boils down to connecting to the data source (usually multiple data sources), handling the data, and finally using graphical components to create dashboards. A Power BI project has the extension "pbix," and can be opened on any computer that has the tool installed, however, the most interesting way to share the project is to publish it in the Power BI service, being necessary in this case a corporate account.

With Power BI, you can unify all data in an organization, whether in the cloud or locally. Through Power BI gateways, you can connect SQL Server databases, Oracle, Services frameworks of Microsoft Analysis, data from social networks, and other data sources, all in one pane, as will be presented in the topic below.

Data collection and modeling

As already mentioned, the Desktop version of power BI facilitates data discovery by incorporating data from a wide variety of information source sources. The following is the relationship to the currently available data source connection options grouped by category:

- File Category: Excel, CSV, XML, JSON, Text, and directories.
- Database Category: Microsoft Access, PostgreSQL, MySQL, SQL Server, Teradata, SQL Server Analysis Services, Oracle, SAP HANA, IBM DB2, and Sybase.
- Azure Category: Azure Marketplace of Microsoft, SQL database, Azure SQL Data Warehouse, Azure HDInsight, Azure table storage, Spark (Beta) Azure HDInsight, blob storage Azure, Azure repository Date Lake (Beta), Azure Document Database (Beta).

- Online Services Category: Facebook, SharePoint Online List, Microsoft Exchange Online, Dynamics CRM Online, Salesforce Objects, Google Analytics, Salesforce Reports, appFigures (Beta), Digital comScore Analytix (Beta), MailChimp (Beta), Marketo (Beta), GitHub (Beta), Planview Enterprise (Beta), SparkPost (Beta), QuickBooks Online (Beta), Smartsheet, SQL Sentry (Beta), Stripe (Beta), Troux (Beta), SweetIQ (Beta), Twilio (Beta), Webtrends (Beta), tyGraph (Beta), Zendesk (Beta).
- Others Category: Web, Microsoft Exchange, R Script, Data Feed, File Hadoop (HDFS), ODBC, Spark (Beta), Active Directory, SharePoint List.

The desktop version of Power BI also provides features that assist in the data modeling phase, such as automatic detection and relationships, custom measurements, calculated columns, data categorization, and column sorting. You can also view the data contained in the data source, and you can view the model in a diagram where you can perform structural analysis and, if necessary, create new relationships.

Installing and Running Power BI

As mentioned at the beginning of the article, the focus will be on using the desktop version of Power BI, as this version does not require a corporate account. The link for the free download of Power BI is in the links section. For the installation of the Desktop version of Power BI, the following minimum requirements must be met:

- Windows 7 or Windows Server R2 2008 or later versions;
- 4.5 .NET Framework;
- IE 10 or later version;
- Memory (RAM): From 1 GB available, 1.5 Gigabyte or more recommended;
- Screen: Starting at 1440x900 or 1600x900 (16: 9) recommended. Lower resolutions, such as 768 x 1024 or 800 x 1280, are not recommended, as there are components that display beyond these resolutions;
- CPU: 1 gigahertz (GHz) or faster x86 - or x64 bit processor (recommended).
- The installation method for Power BI is the same as for Windows operating system tools, based on the:

  o Next>

  o Next>

  o Next>

  o Finish concept.

After you install Power BI, when you run Power BI, a welcome screen will appear.

From this screen, you can get data, view new data sources, open existing projects, access the tool forum and blog, and tutorials that can help you learn. To perform the example, click the "Login" button. Once this is done, the Desktop version of the Power BI dashboard build screen will be displayed.

There are three types of views in the Desktop version of power BI: "Report," "Data," and "Relations." The "Report" mode is where we built the information display panel. In "Data" mode, you can view the content of each of the data sources, and in "Relations" mode, you can view the diagram with the data sources used in the project. You can change the display by clicking each of the three icons located on the left screen bar.

The scenario used for example

To better understand how to work with some of the features provided in Power BI, we will use an example whose scenario is described below. Consider that you need to develop a dashboard to track sales of XYZ magazines. The idea is to create a panel similar to the one shown in Figure 3, in which it is possible to track the number of magazines sold by time (year, month, day), geographic location of the stores that sold the magazines, the customer profile, analyzing the data. The number of sales by sex and the number of sales per magazine. Each of the components that make up the panel will be explained in more detail below.

To achieve the proposed objective, it will be necessary to use five data sources:

- Magazine: This repository is responsible for storing the magazines offered for sale, consisting of the following attributes: code, name of the magazine, the category it is linked to and an internet link to the magazine logo;

- Bookstore: responsible for the storage of the stores that sell the magazines, being composed by the attributes: code, name of the bookstore, city, state and the country in which this bookstore is located;
- Customer: responsible for the storage of customers who bought the magazines, consisting of the attributes: code, name, gender and the date of birth of the customer;
- Calendar: Responsible for storing detailed data for each date in the calendar. These details are important for the project, as it allows us to view the data in various formats. This repository is made up of the following attributes: Date, Year, Month, Day, Month Name, Weekday, Weekday, Quarter, Quarter, Semester, Extended Date, Day, and Weekend;
- Sale: responsible for storing the sales made of the magazines, being composed of the attributes: Sale Code, Sale Date, Sale Time, Bookstore Code, Customer Code, Magazine Code, UnitValue, SaleQty.

For the purpose of demonstrating the use of Power BI, a DBMS will not be used as a source of information. Although it is easily possible to connect Power BI to a DBMS, it is not the intention of the author of this article that the reader has to install a DBMS in order to reproduce the example presented, for this reason, two types will be considered in this example different sources of data, and the repositories "Magazine", "Bookstore", "Customer" and "Sale" will be obtained from an Excel spreadsheet, and the repository "Calendar" will be obtained from a .csv file. These repositories are available for download from the XYZ website. It is also important to point out that this is dummy data.

Creating the project

To start any project, you must first indicate in Power BI the source of the data. This is when you connect to the data source to obtain the information that will be used later in creating the dashboard for your presentation. Therefore, you will need to select the option to connect to Excel and then select the option to connect to files in .csv format.

To do this, click the "Get Data" button at the top of the screen, then note that a new window for selecting the data source type will open, select the "File" option and then select the "Excel" option. Finally, click on the "Call" button.

That done, select the file "SalesXYZ.xlsx" in the selection window. In analogy to the database area, each Excel file tab corresponds to a database table, each spreadsheet column to a table field, and each row to the records.

When you select the spreadsheet, a new screen opens where you can mark which tabs (tables) will be used in Power BI. For this example, select all tabs and then click the load button.

Once you have loaded the data, you can view it using the "Data" view type located on the left tab of the screen, as shown in the below Figure. In addition to this button, there are two others for the "Report" and "Relations" features that will be used later.

That done, you just have to embed Calendar data that is available in .csv format. Repeat the procedure to get the data presented earlier, but this time, instead of selecting the Excel font type, select CSV, which is also in the File category, remembering that the file delimiter provided in this example is the tab. After importing, when consulting the data from the table "DimCalendar." Once this phase of obtaining the data sources is completed, the phase of processing the data incorporated in Power BI begins.

Handling table data/dimension "DimCcalendar."
The table, also technically called dimension, "DimCcalendar," needs some treatments; these treatments basically involve the formation and ordering of the data.

To do this, click the "Data" button, located in the left bar of the screen, as already shown in Figure 6, and select the "DimCcalendar" table/dimension. Then click on the tab labeled "Modeling" located at the top of the screen. The goal will be to change the presentation form of the "Date" field from the current format (written in full) to the standard format day/month/ year (dd / mm / yyyy). To do this, once positioned on the "Modeling" tab, click on the "Date" column heading, then on the "Format" menu, select the "Date Time" option, and then the dd / MM / yyyy option.

Another point that needs to be addressed concerns the sorting of the fields "mes_name," "mes_name_brev," and "day_of_week_name." The ordering of these fields is important because if you do not do this when you create a graph showing the total sales per month, the result will be displayed with the name of the months in alphabetical order, not in chronological order. First month August instead of January, same for the day of the week. So, to get around this, click on the "MonthName" column, then click on the "Sort By Column" button and select the "Month" field, as shown in Figure 9. This field was used because it corresponds to the month number in the year, thus ensuring the chronological order. This may seem like a minor detail, but it is critical to good navigation of the data when it is in the dashboard. Do the same for the field "mes_name_brev" and also for the field "day_of_week_name," the latter must be sorted by the field "day_of_week."

Handling data from the "DimBookStore" table

Once these actions are completed in the "DimCalendar" table, it is necessary to handle the data from the "DimBookStore" table. What needs to be done is to add a new column, also known as a field, which will be derived, i.e., a field that is based on the content of other fields, which will be called "ParentState." This field will consist of the concatenation of the field "State" plus the comma character and the field "Country." This is important since there are geolocation components that need to receive the data in as much detail as possible, thus making the signage on the map more accurate. To illustrate the importance of this, consider that a sale has been made in the Federal District. If only this nomenclature is entered, the geolocation component will signal the Federal District in Canada, which is not desired, because the intention was to signal Federal District in the USA. When using the field "StateParents" the problem no longer happens, since it would store, in the case of the example, the text "District Federal, USA," thus making the location more accurate.

To create this field, select the "DimBookStore" table, then click on the "New Column" button at the top of the screen and apply the following formula: StateDads = DimBookStore [Status] &," & DimBookStore [Parents].

Do the same by adding a field called "Localization," which should correspond to the concatenation of the city name plus a comma, the state name, another comma, and finally, the country name. The formula used is: Location = DimBook [City] & "," & DimBook [State] & "," & DimBook [Country].

Handling table data/dimension "DimClient" and "DimMagazine"

After the treatment in the "DimBookStore" table/dimension, it is necessary to treat the "DimClient" table/dimension. In this case, it will be necessary to format the date of birth to the format dd / mm / yyyy, and, for this, we must proceed in the same way as was done in formatting the date in the table. "DimCalendar."

For the table/dimension "DimMagazine," the required formatting will be to change the data category of the field "Logo," in other words, it is necessary to indicate to Power BI that this field, although it contains text, belongs to the category Image URL. By doing so, Power BI will interpret the URL to display the corresponding image; in this case, the magazine logo. To do this, select the "DimMagazine" table/dimension, click on the "Logo" column, then click on the "Data Category: Uncategorized" option and select the "Image URL" option.

Handling data from the fact/fact table

For the fact/table "FactSale," four transformations will be required. Initially, format the field "DataSale" to the format dd / mm / yyyy as previously shown. Then create a new column (field) named: "SaleValue," this field should correspond to the calculation of the "SalesQuality" fields multiplied by the "UnitValue" field. The procedure for how to create a column/field has already been demonstrated previously, and the only difference here is the formula, which should be as follows: SaleValue = (SaleFact [SalesQual] * SaleFact [UnitValue])

Then you need to change the format of the newly created field "ValueSale" and the field "UnitValue" to the currency format in the American standard. To do this, select the "ValueSale" column, then in the format option, select the "currency" option and then the "$ USD (USA)" option, as shown in Figure below. Follow the same procedure to format the "UnitValue" field.

Finally, two measurements must be created in the "FactSale" table. The measures correspond to the fact that it will be analyzed from the perspective represented of each table/dimension previously treated.

The first measure corresponds to the total quantity of copies of magazines that have been sold, and the other corresponds to the total value of sales. To create a measure, simply click on the "New

Measure" button, then add the following formula: TotalQtdSale = SUM (FactSale [QtySale]).

Note that the SUM function that is summing up information is being used, in this case, the field "SalesQuality" in the "SalesFact" table.

Also, note that a measure is not shown as a column but as an attribute. It is quite simple to identify a measure, as they are represented by a calculator icon. Be sure to make sure that the data type of this measure is an integer. To do this, click on the created measurement, located on the right side of the screen, and look at the "format" menu at the top of the screen, which should correspond to the "Integer" type.

Do the same by creating a measure to represent Total Sales Value. The measure should be called "TotalValueSale" and should have the following formula: TotalValueSale = SUM (SaleFact [SaleValue]).

Do not forget to format this measure for currency in the American standard. To do this, select the created measure, which is shown on the right side of the screen, and repeat the formatting procedures for currency in the American standard.

Relating the tables

After the data transformation phase is completed, it is necessary to define the relationship between the tables. This relationship is important because it is from this relationship that data from both the fact table and dimension tables will interact. Power BI can identify relationships with a high hit ratio, but for training purposes, existing relationships will be removed, and new relationships will be created.

To view relationships, click the "Relationship" display type button on the left tab of the screen, as shown in Figure: Types of data display, then remove all existing relationships by clicking on the line representing the relationship and then pressing the delete key.

Once all existing relationships are removed, click and hold the mouse on the "DateSale" field of the "FactSale" table/fact and drag it to the "Date" field of the "DimCcalendar" table/dimension. Then click on the "BookCode" field from the "FactSale" table/fact and drag to the "BookCode" field from the "DimBookStore" table/dimension.

Then click on the "CustomerCode" field in the "FactSale" table / fact and drag to the "CustomerCode" field in the "DimClient" table / dimension. Finally, do the same with the field "CodeMagazine" in the table/fact "FactSale" and drag to the field "CodeMagazine" in the table/dimension "DimMagazine."

This type of modeling corresponds to the star-schema model of a Data Warehouse, in which there is a fact, in this case, the "FactSale" table, with its particular measurements that can be viewed from different perspectives. These perspectives are technically called dimension, and in this example, they are represented by the tables: "DimCalendar," "DimClient,"

"DimMagazine," and "DimBookStore." With that done, you can start mounting the data display panel.

Creating the data presentation panel

As a starting point, you will need to click the "Report" button located on the left side of the window. Next, you need to create a structure that displays the "Year," "Mes_Abrev," and "Date" fields that belong to the "DimCalendar" table/dimension in an organized manner from the smallest level of detail to the largest.

To do this, you will need to expand the "DimCalendar" table located on the right side of the screen, right-click on the "Year" field and then select the "New Hierarchy" option.

Then drag the fields "Mes_Nome_Abrev" and "Date" into the created hierarchy. The hierarchy will make it easier to see information in the dashboard as it will be available in the same order as the hierarchy order you created.

Before starting to create the first chart for the dashboard, it is worth noting that an important configuration place for the elaboration and parameterization of the charts is located in the "Views" box, placed to the right of the screen. Here you can choose the type of graph, parameterize which information will be the axis of the graph, what information will be the value, which will be used as the caption, color treatment, filters, and other features.

The first chart that will be added to the panel will be the grouped column chart, so first click on the chart in question within "Views." Doing so will display a representation of this component on the screen, then drag the "TotalQtdSale" measure from the "FactSale" table/fact to the "Value" gap, and then drag the hierarchy created in the "DimCalendar" dimension to the " Axis."

With this, Power BI will present the data grouped by year. Because a hierarchy was used on the chart axis, you can enable navigation to the lower level of the hierarchy, which in this case is the month (an action called drill-down). To enable drill-down, click the icon represented with a downward-pointing arrow within the chart, as shown in Figure above. In doing so, Power BI will double-click a year column as a drill-down request. Do this, and you can view the data grouped by month. If you do this again, you can view the data grouped by date. To return to the high level, drill-up operation, click on the icon represented with an up arrow.

Other features can be added to the chart, for example, changing column colors by year and displaying the label with the value of each column. To do this, click on the "Format" icon located inside the "Views" box represented by a pencil icon. To change the color, click on the "Data Colors" group and enable the "Show All" option and change the colors for each year.

Also, enable the "Data Label" group to display the corresponding value for each column.

Notice how simple it was to set up a sales quantity-tracking chart from a time perspective (year, month, day). There are other properties that can be applied to the chart, but not to extend the article too much, it is up to the reader to find out how each property works.

Reduce the size of the chart so that you can add the next component to the dashboard, which will be a label with the number of magazines sold and another label with the moving value of sales. The label allows you to visualize a value very objectively, without graphics or any interference other than the value itself.

To do this, click on the graphic component called "Card." After the component's graphical representation is displayed in the panel, drag the "TotalValueSales" measurement to the "Fields" gap within the "Preview" frame, as shown in the next Figure below. If you wish to display the value in currency format, simply click the "Format" button represented by the pencil icon. Within the "Views" box, expand the "Data Label" option, and in the "Show Units" property, select the "None" option. Repeat this procedure, creating a card to display the data corresponding to the "TotalQtdSale" measure.

An interesting point to note about Power BI is that components interact with each other, for example, when selecting any year in the column chart, the number of magazines sold and the corresponding value being represented by the labels are automatically updated according to the selected year. This will be even more noticeable as new components are added to the panel.

This feature is very interesting as it gives the user the ability to interact with the information. Just make sure that the drill-down option is turned off in the grouped column chart so that interaction between components can take place.

Continuing the example, now you will need to create a filter by the magazine, the idea is to add a component that allows you to select which magazine you want to view the information. To do this, click on the "Data Segmentation" component and then drag the "Logo" field from the "DimMagazine" dimension to the "field" gap. For an even more efficient filter, click the "Format" button, represented by a pencil icon, within the "Views" box, expand the "Selection Controls" option, and disable the "Single-Selection" option. This will allow you to select more than one filter option.

Note that the logo image of the magazines is displayed, due to the fact that the field "Logo" has been classified as "Image URL" as shown in Figure: (Overriding the data category from the "Logo" field.).

The next component will be a map indicating the states in which the magazines were sold. To do this, click on the "Spot Map" component, drag in the "Location" gap the "ParentState" field belonging to the "DimMagazine" dimension. In the "Color Saturation" gap, drag the "TotalQtdSale" measure belonging to the "FactSale" fact/table, thus, the darker the state color, the more sales were made, and the brighter we got, the fewer sales.

The fact that the derived field called "ParentState" was created, as shown in Figure: (Adding a new field in the table/dimension: "DimBookStore."), was important to prevent states with equal names in other countries from causing problems with map placement.

The next step is to add another filter, this time to represent the cities where magazine sales were made. To do this, use the Data Segmentation component again. How to use this component has already been demonstrated before, just repeat the procedures using field "Location" of dimension "DimBookStore" for the "Field" gap. By adding this component, you will be able to filter sales by city, allowing even more detailed analysis of the information.

To finish the example proposed in the scenario, we need to add two donut charts, also known as the ring chart. The first to indicate the number of sales by customer gender and the second to indicate the number of sales per magazine. To do this, click on the "Ring Chart" component, then drag the "Gender" field belonging to the table/dimension "DimClient" to the "caption" box, and drag the "TotalQtdSales" measure from the table/dimension to the "Values" box. "FactSale" fact. Alternatively, use the color option as shown in the column chart to set the female color to pink and the male color to blue.

Repeat this same procedure was creating a new ring chart, only this time instead of using the field "Gender," the "Name" field of the "DimMagazine" dimension within the "Caption" gap. This will allow you to view the number of magazines sold by magazine name.

It is important to note that data can be updated at any time. There are two ways to do this, and the first is to update all involved tables at once by using the "Refresh" button located at the top of the screen within the "Base" tab. The second way is to update a specific table; in this case, just right-click on the desired table, and when the menu is displayed, click on the "Update Data" option, as can be seen in the next Figure. To see these features in action, try adding new lines to the "SalesXYZ.xlsx" file tabs, and then follow the procedure presented for the upgrade.

Note that with this dashboard, you can analyze the number of magazines sold from various perspectives such as time, represented in the column chart, where you can drill down from year to month until you reach a date. It is also possible to view from the geographical location perspective, through the map graph and filter component corresponding to the city where the store that sold the magazine is located. It is also possible to analyze sales from the perspective of the customer profile, represented in the example by customer gender.

With this information, you can give the director or manager subsidies to act on a decision he or she needs to make, for example, to increase sales, in which city/state you need to invest in advertising, or through your customer profile. , modify the way you relate to it, or which magazine sells the most, or when you sell more.

In short, data that was spread across one or more different data sources was unified and transformed into information. This information has been displayed on the dashboard through graphical components, which provides a more user-friendly and interactive viewing experience.

Of course, the tool offers much more than was demonstrated in the article. As you can see, Power BI allows you to develop dashboards for tracking information quickly. Even those users unfamiliar with BI concepts can, as long as the data source is available, create their own dashboards independently of IT.

Chapter 4

Installation And Configuration Process Of Desktop Version Of Power BI

This chapter covers in detail what you should keep in mind when installing, configuring, and updating the Desktop version of Power BI from scratch.

Although you already have it installed, we also recommend reading it because we address several configuration tips that will be useful to you.

What are the two installation methods, and which one should be used?

There are two ways in which the Desktop version of Power BI can be obtained:

- **Method - I: Download from the Web.**
  - o Available for any version of Windows after Windows 7.
  - o It is the one that almost everyone uses and is the least recommended by us.

- **Method - II: Install from Microsoft Store or Microsoft Store.**
  - o It is only available for Windows 10.
  - o It is what we recommend that you use because it has some advantages that we will describe below.

Method I: Download from the Web

Minimum System Requirements:

- Windows 7 or higher
- Windows Server 2008 R2 or later.
- 1 GHz CPU or higher.
- Memory (RAM): At least 1 GB available

Enter the link: [https://powerbi.microsoft.com/en-us/desktop/] and click on "Download or Language Options."

Then choose the language you prefer...

Power BI can be installed in English, among other languages.

But since there is much more information on the website in English, we recommend learners from outside of English speaking countries to become familiar with the Power BI concepts in English.

You will have better answers on Google if you have any questions about a specific topic.

For example, if we search for "query in power bi," it yields 6.5 million results, but if we do the same search in Spanish," queries in power bi," we only have 258 thousand (less than 4% of the results).

It is only a recommendation. If you feel more comfortable, you can use it in Spanish without problems.

Well, let's continue...

Once the language is selected, you must click on "Download." Then select one of the two options:

- PBIDesktop.msi - 32-bit version
- PBIDesktop_x64.msi - 64-bit version

To know which version your computer or laptop supports, you must go to the "File Explorer," right-click on "Computer," and on the options, click on "Properties."

There you should look where the "System Type" is if it says 64 or 32 bits.

Choose the appropriate version and complete the download. Remember:

- PBIDesktop.msi - 32-bit version
- PBIDesktop_x64.msi - 64-bit version

When you finish downloading it, install the program...

Accept the terms and then press "Next" on all screens until you reach the last one where you must indicate "Install."

Once you open the program, it will give you the option to log in or create an account in the Power BI service in the cloud.

But to use the Desktop version of Power BI, it is NOT necessary to create an account on powerbi.com so you can create your account later and close the screen to start using it.

And there you are, you already have the program installed.

Now let's look at method 2, which is the one we really recommend.

Method II: Install from Microsoft Store (or Windows Store)

Minimum System Requirements:

- Windows 10 or higher
- 1 GHz CPU or higher.
- Memory (RAM): At least 2 GB available.
- X64 bit architecture

These are the four great advantages of obtaining a Desktop version of power BI from the Microsoft Store:

- Automatic Updates. With this version, monthly updates of the Desktop version of power BI have performed automatically with Windows Update. That is, your version will always be updated.
- Smaller downloads. Microsoft Store guarantees that only the components that have changed from each update will be downloaded to the computer, which allows smaller downloads to be achieved in each update.
- Administrator privileges are not required. This is useful for those who have their computers limited for program

installations and should ask the systems department for permission.

- More language setting options. You can edit the language as another option of the application (instead of choosing it before downloading the program as in method 1). You will also have the option of choosing a language for the interpretation of the model and another for the language in which the columns calculated in Power Query are created.

These are the steps ... Click on the Windows key and search for "Microsoft Store."

Search for "Desktop version of Power BI" …

Click on "Get"...

It will start downloading...

Once the download is finished, click on "Start" …

Once you open the program, it will give you the option to log in or create an account in the Power BI service in the cloud.

But to use the Desktop version of Power BI, this is NOT necessary so you can create your account later.

The trick to getting out of this screen is to click on Already have a Power BI account? Log in and then close the next screen that appears.

Activating New Power BI Features (Preview Features)

Power BI introduces new features (or preview features) every month. But these are not available by default. We will have to activate them manually.

This is because these improvements may have errors, and Microsoft prefers that the default program works without bugs or problems.

A feature may be in a preliminary version for several months, and once tested and improved, it is incorporated into the default software.

To be able to use and test the preliminary versions, you must go to File ➔ Options and Settings ➔ Options and click on the ones you want to try.

It is important that you download the latest version every month and review this step in order to test the new features that interest you.

The 2 alternatives to using Power BI Desktop on Mac computers

There is no version of the Desktop version of Power BI for Mac. Why?

The reason may be:

- Developing the version of Power BI for Mac would take a whole year and would imply stop improving the Windows version, which they are not willing to do.

- As an alternative, they will gradually incorporate the features that are currently only available on Desktop to the Cloud version of powerbi.com.

As they have advanced in the data summits, Microsoft's vision is to provide a 100% functional version in the Power BI cloud.

Today we cannot create or edit queries, DAX calculations, or relationships between tables, but this may be available in the Cloud version in the future, and Mac users can use Power BI directly from the browser.

What do we do in the meantime?

For Mac users, there are two alternatives to use Desktop version of Power BI:

- Installing Windows in a Virtual Machine.
- Install Windows in Boot Camp A native Mac application that installs Windows on a new disk partition. It is the most recommended for performance issues, but you have to have enough disk space. For more information, you can see the step by step in this link [https://support.apple.com/el-gr/HT201468].

Next steps

If you followed the steps, you already have a Desktop version of power BI installed on your computer.

You can now join millions of users around the world who create data models, reports, and dashboards in a much more effective way.

Now is the time to import your data, create a model, and start creating your first reports.

Chapter 5

Getting Smarter With Power BI

B usiness Intelligence changes the way companies conduct their business operations.

Power BI started out as a set of extra tools within Excel, taking data from tables, and helping the user to filter and work this data before making it into useful charts.

Slowly, Power BI has become a widespread web service and an application for any company's computers. In addition, it has consolidated itself as a unique data analysis tool, retaining much of Excel's familiarity with its own enhancements.

Power BI provides a 360-degree view to users
If you need to deliver analytics and report to your company, the Power BI will enable you to be creative and productive. Power BI is a data mashup with advanced features and a reporting tool.

Connect data from different databases, web services, and files using visual tools that automatically help you understand and correct data quality as well as the formatting Points.

Increase the speed of analysis by 10x or more

Over 20 visuals and a community that contributes to custom visualization can create impressive reports that effectively communicate the message. With the Power BI service, you can securely publish the reports to your company and can configure the auto data refresh option, so everyone gets the most updated information.

It is a program that puts visual analysis at your fingertips by creating intuitive reports. Drag and drop content to place it exactly where you want it on the fluid, flexible canvas. Discover patterns quickly as you explore a single, unified view of interactive, linked visualization.

Integrates proven Microsoft technologies - the powerful Query engine, Power View visualization, and Power Pivot modeling.

With the combination of Desktop version of power BI (where powerful data connections, templates, and reports can be created) and Power BI service (where Desktop version of Power BI reports can be shared so users can view and interact with them) with them), new information from the data world is easier to model, create, share, and extend.

Users of this program will discover a powerful, flexible, and highly accessible tool for connecting with the data world and formatting it, creating robust models, and writing well-structured reports.

With it, you connect to data (usually multiple sources data), format that data (with queries that create compelling and insightful data models), and use that model to create reports (which other people enjoy, use and share).

When you have successfully completed the steps (connect, format, model, and view), you can save this work in a file format that has the extension .pbix. These files can be shared just like any other file, but the most attractive way to share is to upload (share) them to the Power BI service.

With it, you centralize, simplify, and streamline what would be an arduous, dispersed, and disconnected process of designing and creating reports and repositories for your business intelligence.

The desktop version of Power BI is free, Microsoft has promised never to charge you for it, so click on the "option DOWNLOAD FREE," provide your data and click on "GET STATED." The file installation will be downloaded to your PC. Install the program by following the steps presented.

Once the installation is done, it's time to start putting all the instructions in this guide into practice. It contemplates the basic operations of the application, intended for those who are beginning to work with the tool, or for those who have seen it once but not yet used it, or do it without any theoretical basis, and it is also for everyone who wants to gain more knowledge. , learn to work with a powerful tool that gets more fans every day.

In the Desktop version of Power BI, you can connect to data from many different sources. To connect to data sources, we have the following ways:

- When the program starts, on the screen Welcome, there is the option Get Data.
- Menu Home / Get Data. Clicking the arrow next to the name "Get Data" will display the Most Common data type menu.
- The next window will appear. This window can also be accessed by clicking on the "option More ..." that appears at the bottom of the "Most Common" list.
- On the previous page, as well as clicking on the "option Get Data" on the Welcome screen.

Connecting to a Data Source

In order to get connected with the sources of data, choose data source from the Get Data window and select Connect, or choose directly from the "list most Common" if the connection you want is already in this list.

- Menu Home / Get Data. Clicking directly on the image above the name "Get Data" will bring up a window with all available data source connection options.

- Also, the option Web can be selected in the Other data connection category like Home > Get Data (Most Common List)> Web
- Depending on where you will be connecting to, there will be a step to enter the connection credentials for the chosen server. A connection-specific window is displayed to the type of data connection used (each connection type will have its own window).
- Select from the list of tables on the left side of the pane Navigator the option "List of Units XYZ American" and then choose Edit.
- You are able to load the data by choosing the Load button simply from the bottom part of the dashboard, or can edit the query prior to load data by choosing the button "Edit Query." Click Upload.

In some cases, simply choose "Anonymous" and click Call. This step is only applied if there is an exceptional condition; otherwise, it will automatically skip to the action next.

Format and combine Data

To give you an idea, Power Query also belongs to heavy artillery in our Excel arsenal; to clean, integrate, standardize and transform data, which can be used in reports or other solutions created directly in Excel or with the help of Power Pivot.

The whole process of Importing, Transforming and Loading data (ETL Process - Extract Transform and Load-) can be done efficiently with Power Query, without having to rely on VBA or matrix functions or other skills that, to be honest, require a lot of practice and only a few users dominate flawlessly.

We will see, the text file does not follow certain standards (Tabular format to give you an idea) since the first row contains information that is not relevant for the analysis, in addition to that, it hinders it. Consequently, it is necessary to make certain modifications...

Import Data to Power Query (Extract) from the Text file
First, we open a new workbook in Excel and go to the Power Query tab. There, in the Get External Data group, we click on the From a File command and select the From Text option.

Note: *For Excel Version, 2013 Power Query is an add-in and is not included in Excel. It must be downloaded, installed, and enabled in COM add-ins. The above differs from the version of Excel 2016 because Power Query becomes a native Excel functionality and is found in the DATA tab, group GET AND TRANSFORM.*

Next, we choose the location of the text file on our computer and press, OK.

Automatically, the Query Editor or the own Power Query interface appears with the table loaded and with certain modifications made.

Query Editor: here, we clean and transform the data table (which is essentially a copy of the source data, created only to facilitate the analysis, so the modifications made are only reflected in the output table and not directly in the origin of the data).

Note: *The name of the default query is the same as the name of the source file; it is an outstanding practice to give it a descriptive name.*

Power Query "intuits" that it is a type of text file delimited by characters; especially, the columns are demarcated by semicolons (;), however, the first row and the last column are not necessary, so we must modify our Query.

Note: *In the Query Configuration panel, we can modify the name of the query or output table that we want to obtain through Power Query, as well as the steps or modifications applied to the initial or source table.*

Transformation in the Power Query Editor

First, we will remove the last column, left-clicking on its label to select it, then, right-click and in the list of options that appears, we choose Remove.

Now, let's go to the Home tab in the Query Editor and click on the Reduce Rows command and then Remove Top Rows.

In the dialog that appears, we specify the number of upper rows that we want to remove, for this case, the first row and click OK.

Additionally, we go to the Transform tab, and in the Table group, we click on the command. Use the First Row as Header and choose the option of the same name.

To finalize the transformation of the data, we will modify the type of format of the Income column, and the Expenses column (Keeping CTRL pressed, we choose the labels of the column Income and Expenses with a left-click -> right-click on some column -> select the option Change Type -> Integer).

And that's all we have to do to clean our data.

Let's pause a moment and see how, in the area of Applied Steps, the modification steps that have been made in the table are saved so that when loading new data at the source, the transformation process should not be repeated, but the only update is necessary the query... something incredibly productive, just think about this. How much time do we spend a month or a week cleaning and preparing data?

Load
To load the table in the data model, we go to the Close and Load command and choose the Close and Load In option.

In the Load In the dialog box, we choose where we want to load the clean and ready table to be used, either directly to the data model ("Power Pivot") or as a Structured Table in Excel, for this case the first option.

That is why we must enable the Create only connection and Add these to the Data Model options, to finish we click on Accept, and this is how easy we load the query into the Data Model.

Create a Dynamic Table Report

To summarize the information and analyze it, we will create a pivot table report using the Query that we have just created: Insert Tab -> Tables Group -> PivotTable -> in the Create PivotTable dialog box we enable the option -> Use an external data source -> We click on the Choose Connection button.

When you press the Choose Connection button, the Existing Connections dialog box appears where you must choose the name of the query and press the OK button.

Again we accept in the Create Dynamic Table Dialog box, and now the area to build a pivot table appears along with the query panel and the field panel of a pivot table.

Now we are going to move to the filter area, the Year field, to the row area the Month field, and to the values area the Revenue and costs fields.

To make the report more robust, we will create a Power Pivot Measure that determines the average income.

Select the Excel Power Pivot tab, Calculations group, and in the Calculated Fields list, choose the New Calculated Field option.

In the Field Calculated dialog box, we will create the measure:

$$= AVERAGE (Revenue [Income])$$

Check the formula and click on Accept...

The new measure appears in the fields panel of our pivot table. Additionally, we will add it to the values area.

And in this way, we have completed the creation of the report, preventing the transformation and preparation of the data from becoming a headache. Additionally, observe how Power Pivot works in harmony with Power Query, an explosive couple!

Dashboards, reports, and datasets are the essence of Power BI
A report is a view from multiple perspectives of your data, with visualization representing different findings and information gained from that data. A report can have a single view or pages full of visualization.

A report from Power BI may consist of single or multiple pages of preview (graphs and charts such as pie charts, treemaps, line charts, and more).

The desktop version of Power BI includes a Report View, where you can create as many report pages as you like with visualization. Report View provides virtually the same design experience as that found in Edit View, a report in the Power BI service. You can move visualization from one place to another, copy and paste, merge, etc.

The difference between them is that by using the Desktop version of Power BI, you can work with your queries and model your data to ensure that your data supports the best ideas in your reports. You can then save your Desktop version of power BI file wherever you want, either on your local drive or in the cloud.

Before we get in fact reports, we will make a small change in the data, adding a column that will facilitate the report preview in Mapmodel, choropleth map, or other visualization based on geolocation.

Adding Columns to a Query
From the Home ribbon, select Edit Queries. Then select the ribbon (1) Add Columns > (2) Custom Column.

Under Available Columns, click Status so that the column will be inserted in the Custom Column Formula this column between two square brackets ([]). In this field, supplement the formula by typing the following: "&," "&" USA "(this will make Power BI identify that it is a region of USA and not of another country).

Note that after doing all these steps the formula syntax was correct and without error, as the message displayed, otherwise the message would be different, warning of some error in the formula. Once you have completed all of these steps, click OK. On the ribbon, Home click Close and Apply.

In the new column names field, insert the name for the column of State,(this name will help identify the Power BI that is related to a state field).

Creating Simple Reports

In view, Reports will create some visualization of the loaded data in this example. To create a view, simply drag a field from the list Fields to the view Report. In this case, let's drag the field State from USA States and see what happens. One will be Table with the pattern created, but we want this vision as Map, so click on the corresponding icon on the Visualization dashboard.

Note that in the fields of the view option Map the column has State been inserted in Location automatically. Each American state got a Bubble, all the same size.

Let's change this view to Choroplectic Map now, then drag the column IDHM 2010 from IDHM to the field Color Saturation, and see what happens. You will notice that states with the best HDI indices are darker on the map, while the worst indices are clearer.

Note that in the Views dashboard, we can select different types of views, and in the area below these icons, we can drag fields to different areas to apply a Caption or modify the view.

Let's create some more graphs and visualizations to enrich the analysis and make a complete report with valuable information for a decision, knowledge, evaluation, monitoring, etc...

Note that the Visualize dashboard, can select different types of views, and the area below these icons can drag fields to different areas to apply a label or change the display

Let's create a few other charts and views to enrich the analysis and make a complete report with valuable information for a decision, knowledge, assessment, monitoring, etc...

Click on the blank area to deselect the map view and now select the Clustered Column Chart. Drag to the Axis column State field StatesUSA, and the field Value drag IDHM 2010 IDHM. Change the size of this chart by the adjustable edges of this view until it is comfortable and good to see.

Click again on the part of page blank and we will now enter a view, Treemap drag the column State StatesUSA to the field, Groupdrag Population (2014) of StatesUSA to the field Values and final column IDHM 2010 IDHM for the field Details, adjust the size of this chart for a better accommodation in the visualization.

In this visualization, we are comparing the state population with the MHDI information for these states entered.

Now drag the column IDHM 2010 IDHM to Fields, the second card select the arrow to drop down in the field below and choose dragged as a minimum, repeating the same process image above, but selecting the minimum option.

Click on the blank part of the page and we will now insert two views Card, in the first one we will put the highest IDHM 2010 index and in the second the lowest index, initially then drag the column IDHM 2010 from IDHM to Fields of the first card, select arrow dropdown in the dragged field as below and choose Maximum.

Adjust the sizes of the two cards to be integrated into the report for the best viewing experience, see below for the final result of creating this Report.

Now just save your work. File > Save. Give the most appropriate name. A file with an extension will be saved, .pibx, and it can be sent to others like any other program file, so anyone viewing needs to have a Desktop version of power BI installed.

There are other possibilities for sharing these files, which can be done through the Power BI service; you can load the file .pbix directly from the Power BI service.

Note: *In chapter 4, we have discussed the installation & configuration process of the Desktop version of power BI service in much broader depth.*

Chapter 6

Power BI And Excel Power Query And Power Pivot Add-ons

Query Editor (aka Power Query)

What is Power Query and how to find it in Power BI
Power BI Desktop Power Query has a built-in module. In the help and interface, this module is called the Query Editor or the query editor. Power Query is the primary data tool in Power BI desktop. As shown in the screenshot below, all four selected buttons are related to the Power Query Editor.

What is Power Query and how to find it in Excel 2010-2013
Also, Power Query is an add-on for MS Excel 2010 - 2013. It is installed additionally. You can download the add-on here. The Ribbon panel in Excel 2010 and 2013 Power Query has a separate tab.

What is Power Query and how to find it in Excel 2016
Excel 2016 Power Query is already integrated. You can find it on the Data tab, the "Get and Transform" block.

What is Power Query and how to find it in Excel 365

Excel 365 Power Query is already integrated. You can find it on the Data tab, the "Get and Transform" block.

Depending on the version of the Excel subscription, the functionality of the Power Query may vary.

Why do you need Power Query

Power Query is needed for convenient data conversion (ETL process).

According to Wikipedia, ETL (Extract, Transform, Load) is a process in managing data warehouses, which includes:

- extraction of data from external sources;
- transforming and refining them to fit the needs of the business model;
- and loading them into the data warehouse.

Power Query is great for tasks:

- connections to various sources (various types of files, API, databases, etc.);
- for convenient and flexible conversion of data into the required format;
- To create repeatable data processing sequences.

What is a query (Query)

The query is a program in the M language, which is a sequence of data processing.

In its body, a query can access an unlimited number of data sources (including other queries). As a result of executing the request, the output is:

- table - table
- value is value
- the list is list
- record - record, etc.
    - o A list of all the queries in Excel can be seen in different places.
    - o In the list of Query Pane Queries from the Excel 2016 interface.
    - o In the interface of Power Query itself.
    - o Each request has its own name.
    - o The request name can be seen in several places. There you can change it.
    - o In the interface of Excel 2016.
    - o In the Power Query interface.

By query name, you can access the results of this query from other queries.

If the request name contains spaces (for example, consists of several words), then when accessing this request from other requests, it starts with #and is enclosed in quotation marks:

"request name"

Actions on requests (by right-clicking on them)

Duplicate (Duplicate)

The Duplicate command allows you to create a new query and duplicate all the steps of the original query in it (i.e., when duplicating, a new query appears with #"Name (2)"all the steps from the original query). A new query created using the Duplicate command has nothing to do with the original query.

Reference

Create a new request, in the first step of which apply by name to the original request.

Step

- A separate stage of data processing within a specific Request.
- The request consists of steps and includes at least one step.
- For each applied action, a new step is created in the interface.
- The list of steps for a specific request can be viewed on the right side of the screen in the Request settings panel.
- Each step is a separate variable located on a separate line of code in the query script in the programming language M.
- To see the formula for a specific step, you must enable the display of the formula bar on the view tab and select the step of interest in the "Applied Steps" panel.
- The sequence of steps can be changed through the interface using the context menu.
- And also by dragging the steps in the list.

Options in Power Query

Loading data from various sources in Power Query
In order to start working with Power Query, you need to get data from some source. You can do this from the Power Query interface in Power BI.

In Excel 2010-2013, you can do this by clicking on the buttons indicating the various sources in the Ribbon panel.

And also from the Power Query interface in Excel.

Assigning data types to columns in Power Query
The data types assigned to individual columns define the operations that apply to them. If you select a column, then the data types applied to it can be seen in the following places:

- In Power BI, data types are indicated by icons in the columns
- In Power BI and Excel, on the Home tab
- In Power BI and Excel, on the Transform tab

Data Types in Power Query
At the time of this writing, Power Query had the following data types:

- Decimal number - decimal number type number or Number.Type
- Time - time type time or Time.Type
- Date – Date type date or Date.Type
- Date / Time - Date / Time type DateTime or DateTime.Type

- Date / Time / Timezone - date / time / time zone type date timezone or DateTimeZone.Type
- Duration - duration type duration or Duration.Type
- Fixed Decimal number - decimal rounded to 4 digits Currency.Type
- Whole number - an integer Int64.Type
- Text - text type text or Text.Type
- True / False - True / False
- Binary - binary code (for example, image in bmp format)
- Percentage - percent Percentage.Type

In addition, there may be structured data types in individual cells in Power Query:

- Table - table #table({"Heading1", "Heading2"}, {{"String1Column1", "String1Column2"}, {"String2Column1", "String2Column2"}})
- List - list {1,2,4} - a list of Numbers elements with values 1, 2, 4
- Record - Record [field1 = "quoted text", field2 = "quoted text2"]

Automatically detect data types for columns

Power Query has an "automatically detect data types" feature. Using this function, Power Query will select the data type to the column on the basis of the first thousand rows of a particular column.

Duplicate Column

- Team at Ribbon
- Command in the context menu

Rename Columns

- To rename a column, double-click on its name

Remove Other Columns - remove other columns

To increase personal efficiency (due to a better focus on specific numbers), to preserve RAM and to support the performance of models, you should leave only the necessary data in the data model (only the necessary columns and rows).

For these purposes, the "remove other columns" command works great.

Split Column by Delimiter - Split a text column by delimiter

The "split column by separator" command can be found in several places:

- Button on Ribbon - Split Column
- In the context menu, by clicking on the column heading.
- Separate column by arbitrary delimiter
- Specify the maximum number of columns

Append - add one table to another table

- From the Power Query interface
- From Excel interface

Merge - connection of the data of one request with another request using a common key (analog of VPR)

- Start of operation from the Power Query interface:
- Beginning of the merge operation from the Excel interface:
- Selecting a table from which we will pull data, determining key columns and type of operation

Compound key data join in Power Query

- After clicking on the OK button, we see a new column with a button
- Click on the button, expand the column and select the desired operation
- Expand - expand data from selected columns
- Aggregate - count data in specific columns

It is important to remember that the data types of the key columns (in both tables) must be the same.

Extract data from files in a folder

- Select the folder as the source type. Next, select a specific folder with files that are supposed to be merged. Files must be of the same type and with the same columns.
- In the appeared data preview window, click on the edit button.

Group by the team (group by field)

- You can call a command by clicking on a button in the Ribbon panel
- You can also call the command from the context menu (if you right-click on the column header)

Adding a New Column in Power Query

To select an action depending on the condition, Power Query uses a structure with an if then else statement.

Example:

if [column1] 0 then [column2] else [column3]

Conditional column

The Add Column Wizard with a conditional value (conditional column) generates a column value according to the specified rules. The Add Conditional Column Wizard can be found in Power Query, on the Add Column tab, as shown in the screenshot below.

For information, the specified conditions in the wizard interface write a script command containing the operators if then else. This means that the first condition in the conditional column wizard will be checked first. This condition will check all sets of values. If results are found that satisfy the first condition, then a value will be assigned to them based on the results of the first condition. For the remaining values from the set, the following condition will be checked. And so on, until all conditions are verified. If no conditions are satisfied for the elements of the set, then the value from the "Otherwise / (otherwise)" field will fall into the conditional column.

When creating conditions, it is important to remember that comparison operations involving type null and other data types return an error as a result.

Changing the data type of a column from text to decimal, if a decimal place is used instead of a semicolon

1. You must right-click on the column heading

2. Select "Change type"

3. And then select "Using locale"

4. Choose a country where a period is used as a separator (for example, USA)

Delete duplicate columns

The "Remove Duplicates" command goes through the selected columns (if the entire table is selected, then throughout the table) and looks at the repeating cells (rows, if the table is selected). If duplicates are found, the function leaves the first unique line that comes across and deletes all subsequent duplicates. You can find the command on Ribbon - Home - Remove Duplicates (Remove duplicates in selected columns)

Or you can find the command by right-clicking on the header of one or more selected columns. If several columns are selected, then all non-unique combinations of values in each separate row in the selected columns will be deleted.

You can delete duplicate rows in the table by clicking on the button in the upper left corner of the preview table.

A similar result can be achieved if you use the "Group By."

Count rows

- Count the number of rows in the current table

Fetching steps in a separate query
- To execute, you need to right-click on a specific processing step. Select the menu item, "Extract previous steps."
- Enter the name of the new query that will be created based on the previous steps

Function Replace Errors in a Column (Replace Errors)
The function is available by right-clicking on the column heading and allows you to replace errors in the column (for example, those obtained after applying the new data type) to the selected value. Please note that as of 2019-07-29, the function is only available when selecting a single column.

Permissions, Formula.Firewall
When working in Power BI, when accessing external data sources like various APIs, errors like OLE DB or ODBC error: [information is needed in order to combine data] may occur

or Formula.Firewall: Query is accessing data sources that have privacy levels that cannot be used together. Please rebuild this data combination

These are errors that arise due to the built-in Power BI Formula.Firewall - a mechanism that ensures that data from Power BI is transmitted only according to the set access rules.

That is, Power Bi is trying to protect us so that we do not accidentally send any data (like a token) to the attacker server.

However, if we work with the API, then we inevitably need to send data to the Internet. Accordingly, in order to not have problems in this process, it is easiest to turn off Formula.Firewall in the Power BI settings. This is done in the Privacy section. You need to select the 3rd item - "ignore privacy level settings."

Power pivot

What is Power Pivot in Excel

Power Pivot is an Excel add-in, which is a quick VertiPaq column database with the DAX query language (often Power Pivot is used instead of VertiPaq). Unlike Excel, the number of lines loaded into Power Pivot is limited only by the size of available computer RAM. The performance of the Power Pivot is many times greater than the performance of formulas in Excel. Power Pivot also surpasses Power Query in performance (and often consumes fewer resources). Query results are available to users in the pivot tables and pivot charts of MS Excel. Thus, pivot tables act as an analytical interface to the data stored in Power Pivot.

What is Power Pivot in Power BI

In Power BI, Power Pivot is integrated as a database to which various visualizations join.

What is DAX

Dax (Data Analysis Expressions) is a programming language used for queries in the VertiPaq database.

Data model

Data model - a set of tables, relationships between them, and calculated measures in a VertiPaq database. Due to its speed, the data model allows you to create instantly recountable measures, which, in turn, will enable you to create interactive visualizations.

Tables

- Tables - a collection of rows divided into columns.
- Each column has a data type (which is usually inherited from the data types specified for columns in Power Query).
- For columns with numeric data types, you can see the sigma icon to their left. And such columns will be summed by default if you add them to the range of values of any visualization.
- If you add columns with non-numeric data types (without a sigma icon) to the value area, then the default operation will be applied to them: count (counting the number of values).
- A list of tables loaded into the data model can be found in the tree of the field on the right side of the Power BI window.
- Each table has a name by which the data of a particular table can be accessed in measures and calculated columns. If the

name of the table contains a space or non-Latin characters, then when accessing the table from the outside, its name is automatically enclosed in single quotes:

    o 'title with space.'

- However, if we quote the table name without spaces, everything will work as intended:

    o 'title'

Dax Functions

Dax functions are similar to Excel functions, with the only difference being that columns, whole tables, or scalar expressions (simple values) are used as arguments, not cells.

The following are used as argument delimiters depending on the locale:

- ";" (and "," for decimal)
- "," (and "" for decimal)

Measures

Only calculated at the time of use. Calculated within the current filter context. It is this property that allows you to build interactive visualizations that are filtered when you click on certain areas of specific visualizations. Although the measures belong to a specific table, they can be transferred to any other table within the framework of the document. Therefore, it is good practice when using measure formulas not to include the name of the table in which the measure lies. That is, instead of 'table' [measure] writing simply [measure.

Quick Measures

The quick action functionality allows you to create complex DAX formulas without writing code. Instead of writing code, you need to configure the desired measure in the graphical interface.

Calculated Columns

They are calculated once during a table update in a data model. Computed columns take up memory space. Computed columns are calculated within the context of the row. Unlike measures, calculated columns can be used to filter and sort tables. They belong to a specific table, and it is better to indicate them in the formulas along with the name of the table, even if Power Pivot allows you not to do this.

Function execution context (Evaluation context)

In Power Pivot, there are two contexts for executing formulas that act simultaneously:

- Filter context
- Row context

This is a massive and complex topic. At the time of writing the training manual, the author did not understand the topic to the level to tell others about it. Therefore, I recommend referring to reliable sources given in the last of this book.

Link tables in a data model
- To link tables in the data model, one of the tables in the key field must have unique values. Columns must also be of the same data type.
- The direction of communication matters. Computed columns can be used to create relationships between tables.

Linking tables by key date column and time-intelligence functions

If the data model has a separate calendar table and if the fact table is linked to the calendar table by the date field, then to create quick measures in the date field, you need to use the column with dates from the calendar table. A column with dates from a table with facts will not work in quick action.

Commonly Used DAX Features

SUM (Column) - Sum of column numbers

COUNTA (Column) - The number of values in the column

DISTINCTCOUNT (Column) - The number of unique values in the column

SUMX (Table, Expression) - The sum of the values of the expression that is executed for each row of the table

DIVIDE (The value of the numerator, the value of the denominator, an alternative if there is an error dividing the numerator by the denominator) - Safe division

IFERROR (Value, Value if Error) - If an error

IF (Boolean expression, value if true, value if false) - If

DAX Contextual Metrics

Clickthrough rate (CTR)

> = SUM (Clicks) / SUM (Impressions)

CPC (Click Price)

> = SUM (Expense) / SUM (Clicks)

Bid (Maximum click price set by the advertiser)Average bid

> = AVERAGE (bid)

Click Average Weighted Bid

> = SUMX (bid * clicks) / SUM (clicks)

Impression Weighted Bid

> = SUMX (bid * impressions) / SUM (impressions)

CR (Conversion Rate Actual)

> = SUM (transactions) / SUM (sessions)

Key phrase: quantity

> = COUNTA (passphrase)

Key phrase: number of unique

> = DISTINCTCOUNT (passphrase)

About absolute and relative metrics in unloading

The formula calculates the average failure rate:

= SUM (failures) / SUM (visits)

If there is no absolute number of FAILURES in the upload, but there is a FAILURE INDICATOR, then for each line with the initial data, the absolute number of FAILURES must first be calculated. To do this, multiply the Bounce Rate by the NUMBER OF VISITS. After that, you will be able to calculate the average bounce rate correctly.

- The same should be done with viewing depth and time on the site.
- A common mistake is to calculate the AVERAGE FAILURE RATE as a built-in AVERAGE measure on the FAILURE RATE column.
- So the average failure rate is not calculated correctly.

Format for displaying numbers in measures and columns

The format for displaying measured values is set for the selected measure, on the "Modeling" tab, in the "Formating" block

Power BI Settings

Background data - allow downloading in the background (Background data - allow data preview)

It is often recommended to disable data loading in the background, in order to avoid performance problems. Related links:

1. Allow Data Preview to download in the Background option in Power Query and Power BI.

2. Branch, in offers, to turn off this setting by default UserVoice.

Applications
Hotkeys for editing DAX formulas

<u>**Basic editing**</u>

Key	Description
Ctrl+X	Cut string (Empty selection)
Ctrl+C	Copy line (Empty selection)
Alt+↑ / Alt+↓	Moves the current line up / down
Shift+Alt+↑ / Shift+Alt+↓	Copy a line and paste it above / below
Ctrl+Shift+K	Deletes a line
Shift+Enter	Add a new line below the cursor
Ctrl+] / Ctrl+[	Increase / decrease line indent
Tab / Shift+Tab	Increase / decrease line indent
Home / End	Go to the beginning/end of line
Ctrl+Home / Ctrl+End	Go to the beginning/end of the DAX formula
Ctrl+K Ctrl+C / Ctrl+K Ctrl+U	Set/remove the single-line comment
Ctrl+/	Set or remove the single-line comment
Shift+Alt+A	Set or remove the single-line comment

Navigation

Key	Description
Ctrl+G	Go to line
F8 / Shift+F8	Go to the nearest / next error or warning

Search and Replace

Key	Description
Ctrl+D	Select the whole word under the cursor; when pressed again, selects similar words in the text
Ctrl+K Ctrl+D	Go to the next matching selection

Multi-Cursor and Selection

Key	Description
Ctrl+A	Select all
Alt+Клик	Add cursor to selection
Ctrl+Alt+↑ / Ctrl+Alt+↓	Add multicursor above / below
Ctrl+U	Remove last cursor selection
Ctrl+F2	Selects all occurrences of a word.
Ctrl+Shift+L	Selects all occurrences of selected text
Shift+Alt+ → / Shift+Alt+ ←	Extend/reduce current selection by line

Power Query: Steroids for MS Excel and Power BI

As we have learned the basics of this tool at the previous part now in this part, I want to talk about some of the features of free and extremely useful but as yet little-known MS Excel add-in: "Power Query."

Power Query allows you to collect data from a variety of sources (such as csv, xls, json, text files, folders with these files, a variety of databases, various api like Facebook open graph, Google Analytics, CallTouch and much more) , create repeatable sequences of processing this data and load them into Excel tables or the data model itself.

And under the cut, you can find the details of all this splendor of possibilities.

Compatibility and technical details

Power Query is available for free for all versions of Windows Excel 2010, 2013, and is built-in by default in Windows Excel 2016. For users of MacOS X, Power Query is not available (however, even without this, Mac Excel is disgusting to the touch and advanced users, including me, most often work with normal Excel through Parallels or running it on a remote Windows machine).

Also, Power Query is integrated into a new business intelligence product - Power BI, and there are also rumors that Power Query will also appear in other Microsoft products. Those. Power Query has a bright future, and it's time for adherents of Microsoft technologies (and not only) to take up its development.

The way Power Query work

After installing the Power Query, a separate tab of the same name appears in the Excel 2010-2013 interface.

First, in the Excel interface, we select a specific data source, from where we need to get it, and before us opens the window of Power Query itself with a preview of the first lines of the downloaded data (area 1). At the top of the window is a Ribbon with data processing commands (area 2). And on the right side of the screen (area 3), we have a panel with the sequence of all actions that apply to the data.

Power Query Features

Power Query has a lot of features, and I want to dwell on some of my favorites.

As I wrote above, Power Query is remarkable in that it allows you to connect to a variety of data sources. So it allows you to load data from CSV, TXT, XML, json files. Moreover, the process of selecting options for downloading the same CSV files is more flexible and more convenient than it is implemented by regular Excel tools: the encoding is automatically often selected correctly, and you can specify the column separator character.

Combining files in a folder

Power Query can take data from a specified folder and mix its contents into single tables. This can be useful, for example, if you periodically receive some specialized reports for a separate period of time, but the data for analysis is needed in a common table.

Text functions

For columns from the text in Power Query, by clicking on the buttons on the Ribbon, you can apply functions such as:

1. Divide the column by character or number of characters. And unlike Excel, you can specify the maximum number of columns, as well as the direction from which to read the characters - left, right.

2. Change the case of cells in a column

3. Count the number of characters in the cells of a column.

Numeric functions

For columns with numerical values by clicking on the buttons on the Ribbon, you can apply:

1. Arithmetic operations

2. Raise to degrees, calculate logarithms, factorials, roots

3. Trigonometric operations

4. Round to set values

5. Determine parity, etc.

Functions for working with dates, time and duration

For columns with date and time values by clicking on the buttons on the Ribbon, you can apply:

1. Automatically detect the format of the entered date (in excel, this is a big pain)

2. Extract in one click the number of the month, day of the week, the number of days or hours in the period, etc.

Unpivot - Pivot

The Power Query interface has the "Unpivot" function, which in one click allows you to bring the data with one metric arranged in columns by periods to a form that will be convenient for use in pivot tables (I understand that it is difficult to write - see an example). Also, there is a function with the reverse action of Pivot.

Operation Merge - Death of the VLOOKUP

The VLOOKUP function is one of the most used functions in MS Excel. It allows you to pull data into one table from another table with a single key. And just for this function in Power Query, there is a much more convenient alternative - the Merge operation. With this operation, joining tables of several tables into one by key (by simple or compound key, when a match must be found by several columns) is performed in literally seven mouse clicks without keyboard input.

The Merge operation is an analogue of join in sql, and it can be configured so that join is of different types - Inner (default), Left Outer, Right Outer, Full Outer.

I have prompted here that Power Query is not able to do Approximate join, but can. True, out of the box, there are no alternatives.

Connection to various databases. Query Folding

Power Query is also remarkable for being able to cling to a wide variety of databases - from MS SQL and MySQL to Postgres and HP Vertica. In this case, you do not even need to know SQL or another database language, because data preview is displayed in the Power Query interface and all those operations that are performed in the interface are transparently translated into the database query language.

And in Power Query, there is the concept of Query Folding: if you are connected to a compatible database (currently it is MS SQl), then Power Query will try to perform massive data processing operations on the server-side and take only processed data to itself. This feature dramatically improves the performance of many treatments.

Programming Language "M"

Power Query add-on is an interpreter of a new, scripted, data-specialized programming language M.

For each action that we perform with data in the Power Query GUI, a new line of code is written to the script. Reflecting this, in a panel with a sequence of actions (area 3), a new step is created with a talking name. Due to this, using the panel with a sequence of actions, we can always see how our data looks at each processing step, we can add new steps, change the settings of the applied operation at a specific step, change their order or delete unnecessary steps. Also, we can always see and edit the code of the written script itself.

The M language, unfortunately, is neither like the formula language in Excel nor MDX and, fortunately, is not like Visual Basic. However, it is very easy to learn and offers tremendous opportunities for manipulating data that are not available using the graphical interface.

Downloading data from Google Analytics and other API

Having mastered the "M" language a bit, I was able to write programs in Power Query that can connect to the Google Analytics APIs and pick up data with specified settings from there. For Google Analytics, there are quite a lot of exporters of this kind in different implementations.

Power Query can generate headers for post and get requests and take data from the Internet. Thanks to this, with the right level of dexterity, Power Query can be connected to almost any API. In particular, for my research, I pull data on phone calls of clients from the CallTouch API, from the Rescuetime computer activity monitoring service API, I am engaged in parsing the web pages I need to retrieve relevant information.

Once again about repeatability and application options

As I wrote above, the Power Query script is a repeatable sequence of manipulations applied to data. This means that once you configure the processing you need, you can apply it to new files by changing just one step in the script - indicating the path to the new file. Thanks to this, you can get rid of a huge amount of routine and free up time for productive work - data analysis.

I do web analytics and contextual advertising. And it so happened that from the moment I met with Power Query in its interfaces I spend more time than in Excel itself. It's more comfortable for me. At the same time, my consumption of another great add-in in MS Excel, PowerPivot, has also increased.

Here are some of the tasks I do use Power Query:

- I analyze the semantics for Thick projects,
- I make frequency dictionaries,
- I create a web analytic dashboard and reports to analyze specific slices,
- Restoring goal achievement in web analytics systems, if they are not configured on the project,
- I smooth the probability forecast by the methods of Andrey Belousov (+ Bayes :),
- I do an audit of contextual advertising on data from K50 statistics,
- And many other different ad-hoc analysis tasks that need to be done only once

A few words about localization

On the Microsoft website for users from non-English speaking countries, by default, Power Query with the interface translated into the user's native language is downloaded. Fortunately, the localizers did not get to the translation into a native of the programming language (as it was done with the formula language in excel), but the lives of users with ambiguous translations made it very difficult. And I urge you to download, install, and use the English version of Power Query, although your mother tongue is not English. Believe me; it will be much clearer.

Chapter 7

Your Data Has The Value Of Gold - Use Power BI To The full Potential To Exhaust

We know that Microsoft Power BI is primarily a business-oriented cloud-based data analysis service that allows you to collect, analyze, and exploit data, and then share the desired information. This Business Intelligence (BI) tool from Microsoft Office 365, allows you to control your business's health through an active dashboard, generate smart interactive reports with the Desktop version of Power BI, and access data anywhere with native mobile applications.

Bring your data to life with Microsoft Power BI!
Power BI can unify all the data of our organization, either in the cloud or locally. In this way, we will have all the information of our company at our fingertips, and with a single visualization, we will be able to evaluate in an easier way the strengths of our company, saving us time and being able to dedicate this one in what is really important.

With the Power BI, we can create panels, graphs, and reports in a personalized way with our data. The creation of a panel is simple and convenient, thanks to the more than 65 connections with well-known business applications, which are completed with panels generated and designed by experts to help us get answers to our questions.

- Make spectacular interactive reports that reflect the state of your company with maximum precision.
- With Microsoft Power BI, you can access real-time information to identify any type of trend in your sector.
- Thanks to Power BI Desktop, you can screen, process, and combine all your data in a simple way.

Microsoft Power BI will help us create and design rich visual objects from our company or business data. It is the perfect tool if what we want is to monitor everything that concerns our company in a very graphic way. In addition, being an online service, Microsoft allows us to create panels and reports and then share them. In them, we can embed graphics, mosaics, images, and long etcetera to make more comprehensive visual, pleasant, and entertaining, the monitoring of your data.

Microsoft Power BI can unify all the data in your organization, both internally and externally, in the cloud or locally.

We can say that with Power BI, we will work differently from everything we know, and we can perform our work routine in a more fun way thanks to this incredible solution.

This exploitation of data, through panels and reports, allows them to be shared by many users of the same company so that everyone can have information about their businesses in real-time, but what types of sources and data can we integrate into Microsoft Power BI?

As we have said before, Power BI can unify all the data of your organization, both internally and externally, in the cloud or locally.

That is, we can use the same information from our own Excel, Dynamics CRM, Dynamics NAV, SAP, Salesforce, MailChimp, Facebook, Google Analytics, SQL Server, etc. As of external data. For example, data collected by the National Statistics Institute, the World Bank, etc.

The wide range of sources of information will facilitate us to have all the information about our company within our reach and in a single visualization. That is, in the past, we can assess the strengths, weaknesses, growths, and opportunities of our company.

In this way, we can save time to focus on what really matters and make the right decisions. That is why it is important to know what results we will obtain with Power BI.

First, it should be noted that, without the need for great knowledge, we can create panels, graphics, and reports to our liking. And so, in a personalized way and with the data prepared, users will only have to choose and drag what type of graphics they want to appear on the panel or report.

In addition, Microsoft Power BI includes Q&A calls. That is questions and answers with natural language. So that only by writing "Madrid Sales 2017", we can see what were the sales of that period and region. And all this, ready to design, build and use the data to get up and running quickly.

Now that we know what Microsoft Power BI is and how it works let's highlight the most interesting advantages and functionalities of this analysis service. There are many and see them all would be impossible, but these are some of the most important:

We can visualize everything that interests us, that is, we can segment our data as we want to get the answer we are looking for, for example:

- Cash flows
- Business opportunities
- Offers
- Orders and their invoices
- Position my clients on a map and find out where they buy more my products and services
- Marketing campaigns
- Objective Tracking

It has a mobile application, that is, we will have our data, graphics, and panels from anywhere to consult them whenever we want.

Creating and designing visual objects from your company's data, without major complications or artifice, is just drag and go.

Microsoft Power BI is licensed per month and consists of online service; that is, we will not need a special infrastructure or make significant investments since everything is in the cloud.

It is the perfect tool if what we want is to monitor, discover, and decide about everything that concerns our company.

The Microsoft Power BI panels provide us with a 360-degree view and collect all the metrics of our company in a single location. The creation of a simple control panel, with more than 65 connections to popular business applications and complete dashboards prepared by experts, will help us work faster and identify any type of trend that begins to be generated in our sector, allowing us to minimize in time possible problems or take advantage of emerging market niches.

In the next parts of this chapter, I would like to link the theoretical explanations with practical application examples. I'll show you what a dashboard or report can look like, and what kind of features and capabilities Power BI offers. So you can get more out of your data in a few simple steps.

The data for our first example I have made available to you online. This makes it easier to follow the individual steps.

In our first example, we deal with common HR KPIs that are used for strategic alignment. We then link these KPIs with Microsoft Flow in a second example. Here's how to seamlessly integrate Power BI into the rest of the Microsoft landscape. In the last part of the paper, we review the services of a smaller company, explaining some components of Power BI in more detail.

Example 1: Improve the processes in your HR department by analyzing, correctly interpreting, and sharing data

In this example, we worked with an Excel folder that is freely available from Microsoft. This data and many other sample data are available online, and you are welcome to "collaborate" while reading. The following link takes you directly to the appropriate data:

https://docs.microsoft.com/en-us/power-bi/sample-human-resources

Imagine we are the HR managers in a big company. In recent years, the company has grown strongly, and accordingly, the personnel costs have increased. The number of employees is also steadily increasing; however, so-called "bad hires" occur again and again (<60 days of employment).

In addition, in times of demographic change, special attention should be paid to the age of employees to see if there is any need for action. Our task now is to gather all essential information and to present decision-makers with up-to-date, clear figures and facts as a basis for decision-making for the reorientation of the personnel strategy. The focus here is to be more effective in the future and to reduce the number of "bad hires."

Preparation of data with Power BI Service

We decide to process the data using Power BI Service. So far, most information has been summarized in Excel lists. These are easily loaded via the "retrieve data" function (retrieve data → files → local files → upload/import). We can then use this dataset to generate the first report.

In the "Fields" tab, which is located on the right edge, we now see the different tables and columns from Excel. In the second tab, "Visualizations," we have the choice of how we want to represent them. Further visualization options are available for free download.

Each displayed field represents a tab in Excel; the sub-items, in turn, represent the table columns of the respective tab.

Data visualization made easy

In the left section of the screenshot, we are shown the various visualization options. In the upper part of the graph, the type is selectable, and in the lower section, you can easily fill this by means of drag-and-drop. It also can be adapted to label and design.

In our case, we want to be the first to see the current number of employees and then to break them down more precisely. To do this, we select the desired graphics and mark in the "Employees" category "Active employees" and set a checkmark next to the "Age group" and "Gender."

Custom, interactive visual elements

The next figure of the HR sample file shows the interactivity of the visualizations. For example, if we are interested in the female quota, just click on the gray "female" side of the pie chart to see the information filtered accordingly.

If you want to view the displayed data in more detail, just right-click on the corresponding graphic. There you select "Show Data." Power PI then returns the absolute employee numbers per age group for the ring diagram, shown in a classic table.

Q & A in real-time

Another important indicator for the HR department is the average age of active employees. In the future, this will be reviewed regularly in order to be able to counteract any risks in good time. To learn this, we use the Q & A feature of Power BI. These are currently only available in English.

Power BI responds to our question, "How old are the employees?" In real-time with a visualization. This is then customizable in shape and style, and we can attach it to the report or to a dashboard. This is served by the small pin needle, which is displayed in the upper right corner of each tile. In addition, we divided the workforce into three age groups to give us an overview. Currently, the ratio of the age groups is balanced. However, as we move the cursor over each section, Power BI opens a bar graph with age by region. This clearly shows that there are individual regions, such as the East, which have to take greater action and, for example, should start with new recruiting and employer branding measures. So the new HR strategy needs to be targeted to specific regions.

Create and organize reports

Thus, we would have a first overview of the current employment situation. Power BI offers the possibility of multi-page structured reports. For logical structuring, it makes sense to create the information for the new settings on a separate page.

The graph on the file shows one way in which the second page of the report might look like. The visualizations show the number of new hires, broken down by age, age group, gender, and employment type. The first tile acts as a filter function, in this case filtering to different regions. Here the region "East" was selected. As the number of new hires has increased disproportionately, the management attaches particular importance to this page.

In the last annual meeting, therefore, a hiring freeze of 15,000 new employees was made for quarters Q3 / 4 2017 and Q1 / 2 2018. This should sensitize the managers more strongly to the topic and should, therefore, be communicated accordingly.

Text fields, other form fields, or background images can help to make the report more concise and appealing.

Similarly, you can add more pages to the report. Our example report is divided into employees, new hires, bad hires, and excretions. In the bottom bar, you can call up these other pages of the report. As already mentioned in the introduction, the number of bad hires should be reduced. For that, we have to take a closer look at the numbers.

An important starting point is a regional distribution. It would be important to recognize whether there are regions that are more or less affected by this problem. The answer is provided by the diagrams above. It is becoming clear that the Northwest region, in particular, is struggling with the problem although she does not employ most of the staff, as the second bar chart shows.

This starting point must definitely be clarified in the dashboard. Maybe the HR department of this region is not well-staffed, needs training or maybe the working environment in these offices is not right. Here must be investigated more closely. An important insight would be to know the reason for the excretion. Most of these bad hires leave the company voluntarily, or will you dismiss them? The following diagram also deals with this question and clarifies the problem. A high proportion of the departing leaves the company at their own request.

The company management also has some complaints about a male-dominated work environment, which they have forwarded to us. Could it be that women, in particular, leave the company faster due to this perception? We also ask Power BI this question, but the answer does not confirm this suspicion. The shares are almost balanced.

Share content - Create a dashboard

We have already worked out some central content. If we want to share these important findings from our report with other people, it makes sense to create a dashboard and share it with the appropriate group of people. For this, we click on one of the graphics to be pinned to the dashboard and select "Tile." Afterward, we can get either dub a new dashboard or pin the graphic to an existing one.

Under "Dashboards," we will now see the created dashboard, by clicking on the three dots opens another menu. This offers the option "release" (Power BI Pro). By entering the email address, the dashboard can be shared afterward.

Example 2: Power BI is not your only Microsoft product? Then use the full potential and connect the tools!

Automate painstaking processes with Microsoft Flow

Power BI integrates seamlessly with the rest of the Microsoft landscape. In one of our past blog posts, we have already introduced the Microsoft Tool Flow. In summary, it is a tool for streamlining workflows. Flow synchronizes data from various apps and SaaS services to automate routine tasks. Flows are uniquely defined by setting responses to different issues. For example, approval processes or the sending of notifications can be fully automatic.

The Power BI data warning makes you aware of critical values in good time

Such a workflow can also be triggered by data in Power BI, more specifically by a Power BI data alert. We have already mentioned this in our blog post. Power BI provides the ability to include warnings on a meter, KPI, or map tiles in the dashboard (both in the app and in the service variant). These warnings are user-specific and therefore are only displayed to the creator even if dashboards have been released.

In our case, we want to keep an eye on the Q3 + 4 hiring numbers. The threshold value is 15,000 new employees, as this will be followed by a hiring deadline according to the annual plan. To create a warning, the corresponding menu must be opened via the three dots in the right corner of each tile. Under Manage Alerts, you can specify all settings, such as the name or determination of the threshold.

Link a data alert to an automated workflow

Then we can connect this warning to a flow. There are two possibilities; either we create a new flow, or we use a template. Here we decide on the second variant. Under "My Flows," we are looking for "Power Bi."

Microsoft now provides us with a selection of different responses to a Power BI data alert. We decide to send an email to a specific target group. In our case, all department heads and corporate management. Other reaction options would be, for example:

- Create a git hub problem
- Raise alert in Microsoft teams

The next step is to decide when to trigger a data-driven alert and what action will follow. We can select the Power BI alert directly from a drop-down list. Then we have to define the group of people and optionally specify dynamic elements such as the URL to the corresponding dashboard. The email content can be further personalized. If these fields are filled out, the flow has been created and will react automatically.

We have decided to give the responsible persons a first reminder about the 15,000 thresholds to send. For this, we have created a second, linked warning for the corresponding value. If the value is exceeded, as, in our example, the warning bell in Power BI displays the number of warnings and opens the corresponding information when clicking.

Microsoft Flow responds immediately and sends the previously defined e-mail. In our case, this contains a short information text, as well as a direct link to the affected dashboard. The sender is Microsoft PowerApps and Flow.

Example 3: Service is important to you? Review performance and capabilities with Power BI

For this example, we worked together with our internal service experts. Based on the most important processes and key figures, we have created a fictitious Excel folder. Numbers and data are fictitious.

In a third example, we want to examine the effectiveness of our ServiceDesk. Our service employees work with the help of a ticket system, which means that requests are recorded as tickets and then processed. When picking up a ticket, both the priority level and the responsible employee must be defined. In addition, each ticket is automatically provided with an ID and assigned to an employee. During the machining process, the employees record customer contact and machining time. If a ticket is closed, the status of success must be assessed and communicated to the customer.

In this year's employee survey, the service department complained about a large fluctuation in workload and capacity bottlenecks. In addition, the service department has a comparatively high fluctuation rate. The management wants to counteract this by improving the planning and workload of the area. For this, it needs the corresponding ServiceDesk data, including evaluation. The goal is to find weak points in order to make the processes more effective. As in Example 1, we opt for Power BI as an analysis tool. This time, however, we are working on the Power BI Desktop variant as a first step and only switch to the service version when the dashboard is published.

Data preparation with Power BI Desktop
After uploading our Excel files to Power BI, we can start creating a report. Above all, we are interested in how many tickets our

customers usually create and how much time they cost the individual employee so that we can better plan their assignments.

However, we want to start with an overview of all 2017 tickets. For this, we want to create a table of all service requests with the respective ID, status, and the requested date. In addition, we would like to have an overview according to customers; for this, we use the visualization type treemap.

Use buttons to create custom reports

Because the graphics interact interactively, we can click on the tile of a single customer, and Power BI provides us with all the tickets for that customer. As the customer base grows, this table will quickly take an intense dimension and is by no means suitable for the specific search. For this reason, we want to offer further filters as restriction criteria, which can be used if required. So that they do not take up unnecessary space, they should appear only when needed. We use a button in combination with a bookmark. Power BI offers predefined buttons, such as the Q & A button, as well as an empty button for your own action definition.

We already created an empty button called FILTER; now, we need to format it more accurately. In the visualization rider, the layout is defined, and other settings can be identified, such as when the button should react. We decide on a reaction when clicking. For our purpose, we then have to turn on the action function in the visualization tab and define the type as a bookmark. Then we look for the right one under the bookmarks and format it accordingly.

Under "View" in the upper menu bar, we mark the boxes "Selection area" and "Bookmark area" and add them to our tabs on the right side of the page. We define the previously selected bookmark after creating all

Graphics so that it only shows us in the selection area those visualizations that we want to get when clicking on the button. This setting can be made in the "Selection" tab.

Make data search easy - install filters
We want to add two additional filter functions. Once, the user should be able to filter the date of receipt of the ticket and second, and there should be the option to categorize with the help of the appropriate abbreviation for those responsible.

In order to be able to consider the date of receipt, we want to offer a slider with which the period can be limited. We add this via the visualization type

"Data cut" added.

Through the Marketplace, Power BI offers additional, free visualization types, and we have chosen the "Text Filter" as the second filter option. The text filter provides the opportunity for a detailed search, in our case, for an employee code. You could also choose a drop-down list instead, but for many people, it will be much too long.

Now we click on the filter button, it will change color, and the two filters on the right side will appear.

Another way to use filters already exists when creating reports or graphics. If you do not want to use all values for certain data, click on the three dots after the corresponding field, and select "Add filter." In this menu, it can then be selected, for example, that only data greater than 0 or similar are used.

Break down, analyze and use data

The next graphic shows us the number of tickets by the customer. Preceded by a filter box, so we have the opportunity to show only dissolved tickets, the unsuccessful or even those for which no final information was deposited. There are big differences. If we move the cursor over the columns, the exact numbers are displayed. The Becker OHG is the front-runner with 72 tickets, whereas the Beinert KG has opened only 4. A comparison with the customer data shows that Beinert KG was only acquired as a customer in November. The same applies to Jung GbR, which has only been part of the customer base since October.

Nevertheless, the Becker OHG lifts with more than ten tickets from other long-standing customers, and there could be various causes. Are the employees on-site possibly under-trained? We check this suspicion and have the average customer contact per ticket displayed. This is relatively small and does not confirm our suspicions.

Here, we need to search the conversation with the service staff to find out the reasons for the increased requests. We may even be able to engage our sales department, which offers the customer a system improvement.

Give orientation with additional lines

Since our service employees have mainly criticized the fluctuating load factor, we are interested in the time distribution of the tickets. Power BI automatically sorts the selected line graph in descending order. Via the "Format" tab, you can insert different orientation lines. Here we have decided on an average line, which is shown in dotted lines in the lower graph.

It can be seen that the required service capacities are indeed subject to strong fluctuations. In the detail view (right-click "Show data"), we see that June is burdened almost twice as much as the beginning of the year. The end of the year, December and November, has much more service needs than the summer months of July, August, and September. One possible explanation would be that many of our customers have company holidays over the summer months, whereas most new customers are won in the fall. These data must be taken into account in future capacity planning. One possibility would be to support the team at the end of the year and at other critical moments with external forces.

Calculate with Power BI averages

We have already talked about possible measures to relieve our employees, such as recruiting temporary employees. Furthermore, we also want to increase the effectiveness of the processes. For this, we take a closer look at the interfaces, in this case, the contact with the customer. In our Excel list, the employees had to fill in the number of required contacts (telephone, email, personal). Since the ticket admission and the conclusion are fully automated, this contact does not count. The value 0 thus represents the optimum.

In our stacked bar chart, we again draw an average line; this is at the value of 1.3. For our bars, we can choose in the visualization rider under the category "value," which values we want to display, here we select "average values." In this way, we obtain the respective average value for each category (customer). It quickly becomes apparent that Becker OHG, the number one ticket holder, with 0.65 contacts per ticket, is well below the average. The Maars mbH opened comparatively only very few tickets, scored the highest value. On average, three tickets (rounded up) will be required per ticket. The question is how to reduce these values. A possible

The starting point would be the drafting of guidelines and the corresponding communication in the customer company, in which specific content must be specified when opening a ticket. Maybe you could also change the system so that incomplete tickets cannot be sent anymore, but the customer receives an error message.

From the generated report can then, as described in Example 1, easily create a dashboard. But you have to change to the service variant. This dashboard should only contain the essentials, as it is limited to one page. For more detailed questions, just click on the appropriate graphic to get to the more detailed report. Dashboards are less flexible in design, and tiles have certain minimum sizes, and also font and color can be adjusted only limited.

In our example, we have shown only the general numbers on the dashboard. This includes the average customer contact as well as the average processing time of a ticket. Since both records have some outliers, we also show them as a line chart.

The bottom tile on our dashboard covers how much time the launch process takes from ticket receipt to editing. Power BI offers the possibility of displaying different values for a data record within a graphic. For example, the average, the minimum, the number, the standard deviation, etc. A start time of 27 days is, of course, not optimal and must be avoided. Here, the system must be critically examined, and tickets can be left behind or forgotten? A possible solution would be to set a workflow, more specifically, to send a reminder email if no start date has been recorded three days after the ticket receipt.

In summary

Power BI can help you cope with increasing data volumes in the business world and keep track of all-important numbers. With Microsoft Power BI, you can bring together and analyze your various data sources in a single dashboard.

With just a few clicks, you benefit from intelligent, interactive evaluations and can answer your questions in real-time. With real-time updates and compatibility with various devices, you do not lose track of things even when you're on the move, and you can always share the most important information with colleagues.

Chapter 8

Microsoft Power BI In A Nutshell

T he Office products from Microsoft are among the most popular applications worldwide. True to the motto "often copied, never achieved," the software convinces with user-friendliness and functionality. More and more, Microsoft is also doing well in business applications. With a long experience in the field of BI with different products and strategies, Microsoft launched Power BI in 2015, a powerful data analysis tool for self-service BI.

What distinguishes this solution and how it can be used can be found in this first newsletter. This will now appear every three months and will be sent to you on request.

Much power for business analytics

Modern BI applications need the power to process large amounts of data quickly and flexibly. But that alone is no longer enough today. More and more users wish that they can flexibly and independently analyze and visualize their data and that the insights gained can be shared with other employees or teams. Presentation in presentations or websites is no less important. Last but not least, many different data sources need to be integrated. All this can be easily handled with Microsoft Power BI, without detailed IT or programming knowledge.

Integrated Microsoft solution components

The solution suite of Microsoft Power BI consists of:

- Windows desktop application, the so-called Power BI desktop, to create new reports.
- Online service, called Power BI Service, on which the generated reports can be published and shared.
- Mobile apps for Windows, iOS, and Android, the Power BI apps, for on-the-go access.

Those who are already on the road with Office 365 are ideal for integrating the components. Power BI uses common user administration and the structures that already exist in O365. In addition, tools such as MS Team, SharePoint Online, or One Drive seamlessly integrated.

Of course, the start with Power BI without O365 is easily possible; all structures and authorizations can also be defined and used within Power BI - of course, with full functionality.

Frequently asked questions by Power BI customers

➢ *I have read the newsletter and would now like to try Power BI myself. What do I need exactly to get started? Is my existing Office 365 account sufficient?*

You do not even need an Office 365 account. Power BI Desktop, the tool needed to create Power BI Reports, is available for free download from the Microsoft website. If you then want to publish the generated reports to the Power BI service, you can still activate the Power BI Service license via your Office 365. This comes in two forms, therefore, the "Free" license and the "Pro" license. Both can be activated in the Office 365 portal with just a few clicks.

If you do not have an Office 365 license, you can easily register the Power BI license with your existing mail address.

➢ *Recently I heard about the "Power Platform." Is this the same as Power BI, or where is the difference? That's really complicated with these terms ...*

Unfortunately, Microsoft really does not make it easy for us with the terms. The so-called "Power Platform" is the central building block of the new world of business applications from Microsoft. It currently includes four components, Power BI for data analysis, PowerApps for creating specialized applications, Flow for designing and automating processes, and Integrated Data Service (CDS) Database.

The goal of this platform is to make as many manual steps as possible while eliminating complexities. As a result, business users are also able to build reports, apps independently, or flows without relying on IT developers or their explicit help. Due to the absolutely seamless integration of the modules, for example, a controller can build its own app for data input with a few mouse clicks and then re-evaluate and visualize this data directly with Power BI.

> ➢ *...if so, I do not need my DWH anymore, right?*

Unfortunately, this question cannot be answered quite generally. Thanks to the many connectors and the extensive "Data Wrangling" functionality, Power BI already has everything it needs to evaluate and visualize data. But this simplicity also has certain limitations. Once complex data harmonization transformations are needed, historical accuracy and traceability of data are required, or a cross-functional analytics platform with appropriate governance is created, a pure Power BI solution is probably no longer the best way. Of course, this does not mean that Power BI cannot still be used as a visualization tool in such cases, but the database is ideally a full DWH system in this case.

> ➢ *And how long does it take to get an attractive first dashboard? Do I have to be able to program this?*

Of course, that is very different. In general, however, it can be said that even less experienced users can already build a very respectable report or dashboard in two to three days. If extensive data manipulations or complex calculation logics still have to be installed, experience shows that it takes a little longer. Programming skills are not necessary at first because Power BI was explicitly developed for the business user. Power BI, however, offers with "Power Query" or "DAX" two integrated languages for data manipulation, respectively. Definition of key figures and other logics. The latter, "DAX," offers a very large range of functions and is very similar to the formula language of Excel, so that people with Excel skills can find their way around Power BI very quickly.

➢ *If I still want to share this with my colleagues, how does it work?*

Sharing a report with others in your own organization as well as in other organizations is easy. After creating the report in the Desktop version of Power BI, it is very easy to publish it on the cloud portal service of Power BI with just a few clicks. Using the Power BI service, you can then make the report accessible to other people by either releasing the individual report for them or by inviting the people right into the workspace, the folder, as it were. All of this is done through the people's Office 365 account, so it's enough just to enter the email address of the recipients, and they will automatically get access to the report. Of course, as a report creator, you can decide whether other people can only view or even edit the report.

➢ *So many features? That's definitely expensive and needs a lot of performance, right? Which servers do I have to order for this?*

That's the attractive thing about Power BI. You can get started right away and create reports based on your data. The creation tool, Power BI Desktop, is available to all for free and can be downloaded from Microsoft's website. To publish the reports to the Power BI service, you need a corresponding license, which can be assigned to you in just a few clicks via the Office 365 portal. This is already available for $ 9.90 per month and user. You do not need any additional hardware, Power BI is primarily a cloud service, meaning that the portal runs in Microsoft's data centers and you do not have to worry about your own infrastructure.

Consistent data analysis

The reality in companies is a variety of different systems and data sources, i. In addition to the core ERP, there are also subject-specific applications such as CRM, various planning Excel, or other special applications. The order of the day is thus the automated connection of the data sources, the production of a consistent data view, and the subsequent evaluation by means of an attractive and meaningful visualization. For simple to medium applications, these activities can be done directly within Power BI. Thus, Power BI makes it possible to transparently structure the entire process from analysis to publication, release, and processing.

There are still good reasons to set up centralized data management, for example, in the form of a data warehouse. These include, for example, the construction of data history, complex integration rules, or very large amounts of data.

Conclusion

Once Again, What Is It About?

With Microsoft Power BI, you can easily connect to hundreds of data sources, present your data with live dashboards and reports, and share them with your organization in the simplest way.

With Power BI, you can create rich interactive reports with visual analytics, gain additional insights from your data, and get even better decision-making to drive the business. It is an excellent combination of tools that can easily connect us to a lot of data sources using the tools of business analytics. Power BI simplifies data preparation, and streamline ad hoc analytics. With Power BI, you can retrieve data, create data relationships, and enrich data models, create reports, save reports, and upload or publish reports.

Find the perfect solution for your company and find the right industry solution for your business.

Industry Solutions (Box)

Power BI turns industry data into smart decisions

Your industry generates a massive amount of information every day. Do you use this data for your company? Find the right industry solution for your business or profession.

- Retail
- Insurance
- Manufacturing
- Aviation
- Services
- Consumer Goods
- Telecommunications
- Energy
- Public Sector
- Capital Markets

For whom?

Microsoft Power BI is the ideal and comprehensive data preparation and visualization solution for all companies who want to take advantage of the cloud at the same time. Generating and publishing enterprise-wide reports across the web or on mobile devices has never been so easy. The data is always available, and every single user can design individual dashboards with a 360° unique view of the business. The dashboards scale enterprise-wide, providing integrated control and security.

For analysts

Realize the insights gained from the data quickly. Within minutes, you can connect to hundreds of data sources, easily prepare the data, and generate reports.

For IT professionals

Develop a data culture that includes everyone. Help your employees work with trusted tools to gain insights within seconds. At the same time, you can meet the requirements for security, control, and regulatory compliance with a trusted enterprise BI platform. Your users can easily access all the necessary data. The benefits for you: easier administration, reliable compliance, and maximum data security.

For developers

Increase the potential of your apps with data. You can easily embed interactive data visualizations and create attractive reports - with perfect visualization on any device.

Your benefit?

- Easy administration, reliable compliance, and maximum data security
- Central access control to company data
- Only power users need to be licensed, View licenses for employees are free
- Free data gateway for local data access
- Installation on up to five devices (per user)

- Get started thanks to the familiar office interface and integration with Office 365 as well as other services from Microsoft quickly
- Improved collaboration and easy sharing.

What about the following specific suggestions for your own Power BI project? Maybe you work in an SME, a larger company, an agency, or an organization. To optimize business processes and to open and conquer new markets, you need insights from existing data.

With Power BI Desktop, you can quickly run reports from a variety of local and web-based data sources. Familiarity with Microsoft products simplifies the creation and processing of the desired reports. Thanks to the integrated visuals, they look really professional with little effort. If you work in a team or want to share your insights with supervisors, you can share your report with the people you want-within the familiar Microsoft Office environment. Incidentally, this also works with people outside the company.

In our next Power BI books (intermediate and advanced), we would be happy to show you how to use Power BI in a more sophisticated way for your company or department based on your own data.

Learning by doing
Now it's your turn. Just try it yourself. Open Power BI online or the desktop variant, download sample data, and create your own reports or dashboards.

Reference

https://powerbi.microsoft.com/en-us/blog/

https://powerbi.microsoft.com/en-us/power-bi-embedded/

https://powerbi.microsoft.com/en-us/power-bi-premium/

https://docs.microsoft.com/en-us/power-bi/service-premium-faq

https://www.sqlbi.com/

https://exceleratorbi.com.au/exceleratorblog/

https://www.kasperonbi.com/

http://prathy.com/

https://datachant.com/?s=power+bi

https://powerbi.microsoft.com/en-us/blog/

https://insightsquest.com/category/power-bi/

http://www.thebiccountant.com/category/power-bi/

https://dataveld.wordpress.com/tag/power-bi/

https://sqlserverbi.blog/category/power-bi/

https://www.powerbitutorial.org/

www.ingramcontent.com/pod-product-compliance
Lightning Source LLC
Chambersburg PA
CBHW071133050326
40690CB00008B/1447